Washed and Well-Fed

Washed and Well-Fed

How the Sacraments Change Everything

C. FRANKLIN BROOKHART

RESOURCE *Publications* • Eugene, Oregon

WASHED AND WELL-FED
How the Sacraments Change Everything

Copyright © 2021 C. Franklin Brookhart. All rights reserved. Except for brief quotations in critical publications or reviews, no part of this book may be reproduced in any manner without prior written permission from the publisher. Write: Permissions, Wipf and Stock Publishers, 199 W. 8th Ave., Suite 3, Eugene, OR 97401.

All scripture quotations herein are from the New Revised Standard Version Bible, © 1989 by the Division of Christian Education of the National Council of Churches of Christ in the U.S.A. All rights reserved.

Resource Publications
An Imprint of Wipf and Stock Publishers
199 W. 8th Ave., Suite 3
Eugene, OR 97401

www.wipfandstock.com

PAPERBACK ISBN: 978-1-7252-8741-9
HARDCOVER ISBN: 978-1-7252-8742-6
EBOOK ISBN: 978-1-7252-8743-3

01/04/21

Dedicated to the Rev. Dr. Kate Cress, Rector, and the People of the Church of St. James-in-the-City, Los Angeles.

Contents

Acknowledgments		ix
Introduction		xi
1	Christ, the Original Sacrament	1
2	The Heart of the Matter	4
3	The Necessity of Complexity	7
4	Begin at the Beginning	11
5	Push the Pause Button	15
6	Soaked in Scripture	18
7	Let's Begin Again	23
8	Not OK	26
9	The Body	30
10	The Best Gift of All	33
11	The God We Fear	37
12	Christ's Story, My Story	41
13	Shifting Gears	45
14	More Covenant	47
15	Remember to Remember	53
16	I Give You Myself	57
17	The Secret Revealed	62
18	Sacrifice	66
19	What Is at the End of the Road?	71
20	The Family Meal	74
21	Food for the Journey	78
22	Thank God!	81
23	Revealed in the Breaking of the Bread	85

Acknowledgments

I WISH TO ACKNOWLEDGE the kind assistance of the Very Rev. Kurt Dunkle, Dean and President of The General Theological Seminary, New York City, in the writing of this book. He provided accommodations and opened for me the extensive resources of the Christoph Keller Library. I am very grateful for his hospitality, his leadership, and his friendship. I also thank Patrick Cates, Library Manager, and Melissa Chim, Reference Librarian, for their warm welcome and helpful assistance.

I would be gravely remiss if I did not also acknowledge the support and help of my wife Susan. She inspired me to write and has always supported and encouraged me. She remains the love of my life.

Introduction

GOD SPOKE. AND THAT changed everything. That is what the creation story in the first chapter of Genesis tells us. The world was chaos, without form, empty. Then God spoke, and that speech formed the world. From chaos to order, from emptiness to a creation full of life and beauty, from formlessness to symmetry and stability.

God acted. That changed everything. The first chapter of John's gospel proclaims that the Word of God became flesh and dwelled among us. The very thing that God wanted to say to the cosmos, the very idea that was most on God's mind, that Word became a human being named Jesus. And consider what Jesus did. He healed the sick, fed the hungry, raised the dead, freed the afflicted, and spoke good news to the poor. What Jesus said and did looked just like what God would say and do. Then Jesus accepted the way of the cross to show how completely God was committed to humanity. And three days later Jesus was raised from the dead by God's power as victor over all that separates God and humanity. God acted, and that changed everything.

But where does that leave us? Is there a place for us in God's story? Does God speak and act on our behalf? The good news of the gospel is a resounding Yes. Whenever the story of Jesus is proclaimed God speaks and everything changes.

When does God act? God acts in many ways, of course. But God has promised to be present dependably and to encounter us fully in the sacraments of holy baptism and holy eucharist. And

INTRODUCTION

when those two sacraments instituted by Christ himself are administered, everything changes.

In this book I aim to carry out two tasks. First, we will explore some of the various meanings and implications of the gospel sacraments. This will not represent a complete treatment of the topic. To do that would turn this into a book of generous proportions. Rather, I want this to offer an accessible treatment of baptism and eucharist in such a way that readers can both comprehend and live into the new life of Christ that is offered in the sacraments. If we know what happens to us in baptism and in the eucharist, we can, I firmly believe, be more deeply connected to Jesus and live more fully as his disciples and his servants in this troubled world. In other words, the sacraments change everything about us. First, I hope you will be enabled to understand what is happening in these two sacraments and, second, be empowered to undertake living into the abundant life offered in and through them.

I write as a bishop of the Episcopal Church, but what I offer I hope will be helpful to any Christian or any person considering taking on the commitment of following Jesus. I present what I believe to be a broadly catholic and scriptural view of the sacraments and how to live into them. My basic authority will be the Holy Bible, but I will also draw on other resources.

Diamonds fascinate us. Who can resist turning one to allow the light to shine from each facet? I hope this book will allow the reader to look at various facets of the gospel sacraments, remembering that real value lies in the stone, in Jesus Christ. I hope you will discover more about Crucified and Risen Lord and thereby be enabled to love him more. The sacraments along with scripture and prayer are the basic ways we are pulled into the life of our Lord. And it is with him that we find life, hope, purpose, freedom, and joy.

We have some important things to consider. Let's set forth in the name of Christ. And expect to be changed!

1

Christ, the Original Sacrament

WHEN I WAS A child and had come down with an illness my mother would look at me and say, "I know what you need." Several hours later a wonderful lemon pie would appear. That delicious confection carried my mother's love, concern, and prayer just as clearly as any word. She was right. It was just what I needed.

Sometimes we need more than words and thoughts. Sometimes we need actions and objects that can help us dive deep into ourselves.

Now think of the soaring prologue to John's gospel. "In the beginning was the Word, and the Word was with God, and the Word was God. He was in the beginning with God. All things came into being through him, and without him not one thing came into being. . . ..And the Word became flesh and lived among us, and we have seen his glory, the glory as of a father's only son, full of grace and truth" (John 1:1–3, 14). The term "Word" overflows with meanings. It connotes what is on God's mind, what God wishes to impart to us, what God would communicate if God addressed us, and even what constitutes the structure of God's mind. That Word took on "flesh," the fullness of humanity, and lived among us. That Word is Jesus.

Moreover, in Matthew's gospel Jesus is given the title "Emmanuel," which means "God with us" (Matt 1:23). And in the

Nicene Creed we weekly recite that Jesus "for us and for our salvation...came down from heaven: by the power of the Holy Spirit he became incarnate from the Virgin Mary, and was made man." The Creed uses the theological word that sums up all this, *incarnation*, being made a human being in every sense.

So now we can say it. Jesus Christ *is* the original sacrament.

But in saying that we need to be clear about a working definition of sacrament. A resource used by many people is the Book of Common Prayer of the Episcopal Church. In the catechism contained in that book we find this simple and widely accepted description: "The sacraments are outward and visible signs of inward and spiritual grace, given by Christ as sure and certain means by which we receive that grace" (BCP, p. 857). Remember that grace refers to the unmerited and freely given favor and blessing of God. Note especially that sacraments use outward means, signs and symbols that carry and convey the grace of God to us.

I have used the term "gospel sacraments," referring to baptism and eucharist. These are the two acts directly commanded by Christ. The outward signs he set aside were water for baptism and bread and wine for eucharist. Over the centuries the church under the guidance of the Holy Spirit developed five other sacraments, sometimes called sacramentals or minor sacraments. These are confirmation; marriage; reconciliation, also called sacramental confession of sins; ordination; unction or anointing with holy oil for healing. In this book we do not consider these five, even though the use of them can be transforming. Rather we will focus on the two instituted by Jesus himself, the two that the church has generally considered necessary for salvation.

Allow me to add to the above definition of sacraments. They consist of 1. outward signs, 2. put into action, 3. with words that add meaning to the action. Additionally, the Risen Christ uses these signs as a primary way to encounter us, to meet us at a deep level of our lives, and thereby to give us his favor, presence, and resurrection life. The gospel, that good news proclaimed in the Bible, is that Jesus' incarnation, ministry, death, and resurrection demonstrate God's deep desire to love and bless us. In short, the gospel sacraments *are* the gospel in action. If this is true, then Jesus himself fulfills the definition. He is the original sacrament of God's grace.

Consider a couple falling in love. They can say to each other, "I love you." Or they can kiss each other. It is the same life-changing message conveyed in two ways, words and acts. Consider the sacraments as the kiss of Christ for us.

But Jesus himself led the way. Christina Rossetti wrote a simple and moving Christmas hymn.

> Love came down at Christmas,
> Love all lovely, love divine;
> Love was born at Christmas:
> Star and angels gave the sign. (*The Hymnal 1982*, number 84)

Does that not change everything?

Review: Jesus is the outward, fully human means of God giving divine love to humanity, so that we can declare that Jesus is the original sacrament.

Discussion question: If Jesus is the Word made flesh, how is your view of what it means to be a flesh-and-blood human being altered? How is your view of God altered?

Action item: Try writing another verse to the hymn quoted above.

2

The Heart of the Matter

IN THE LAST CHAPTER we rooted the idea of sacrament in the incarnation of Christ. We find the Bible's great declaration of this in chapter one of John's gospel: the Word became flesh and dwelled among us. In this way Jesus represents God's foremost sacrament, the living embodiment of God's steadfast love for each and all of us.

Let's dig deeper to discover more riches. One of the traditional ways we express the concept of incarnation states that Jesus was both fully human and fully divine. Christians call this the two natures of Christ. The Nicene Creed, that ancient and basic statement of Christian belief, frames it in the precise language of fourth century Greek philosophy: Jesus is "eternally begotten of the Father, God from God, Light from Light, true God from true God, begotten, not made . . . by the power of the Holy Spirit he became incarnate from the Virgin Mary, and was made man."

I suspect this doctrine began with the reactions of the earliest followers of Jesus to him. They may have said, "To be with Jesus seems to put us in God's presence. And look at the things he says and does. Only God can do that." In today's language we can look at the gospel record of Jesus and the early Christian witness to him and make our own declarations. He seems to be the only person ever fully integrated into God. He is the spotless mirror image of

The Heart of the Matter

the Holy One. He is completely transparent to God. He fully embodied the divine.

All of this is hinted at in Jesus' acts and teaching, but it all comes into clearer focus when we consider Jesus' death and resurrection. When we imagine Jesus hanging on the cross and when we sense that he is God's unique agent we witness the divine entrance into all the pain, tragedy, and sorrow experienced by human beings. On the cross we watch God embracing all the agony and anguish of the world and making it God's own. And that tells us something tremendously important about God. From the cross we learn that God is utterly and completely committed to us. The worse things we can experience cannot separate us from God's desire to be in communion with us. The phrase the Old Testament most often uses to describe God's nature is "steadfast love." The cross stands before us as the supreme sign of this.

The cross, however, does not end the story. On the third day after his crucifixion Jesus was raised from the dead by God's power. Easter represents the victory of the life and love of God over all that stands in the way of the abundant, full life God wills for us. St. Paul puts it this way: "I am convinced that neither death, nor life, nor angels, nor rulers, nor things present, nor things to come, nor powers, nor height, nor depth, nor anything else in all creation will be able to separate us from the love of God in Christ Jesus our Lord" (Rom 8:38–39).

The short-hand phrase that summarizes this is: paschal mystery. The term "paschal" was the early Christian term for Easter. And the word "mystery" suggests something about God that we cannot fully understand even while it pulls us into a deeper understanding of God. The dying and the rising of Christ, that is the paschal mystery. Who can explain it? Yet it calls to the very depths of our lives.

With this in mind, we are ready to return to the discussion of the sacraments. The point I wish to make is this: the sacraments allow us entry into the actuality of the paschal mystery. As we shall discuss later, baptism unites us to the death and resurrection of Christ. And the eucharist functions as meal in which we remember

Christ's death, proclaim his resurrection until the end of time, and receive his risen presence in the consecrated bread and wine.

The Crucified and Risen One had become the paschal mystery in his own person. And in the sacraments he encounters us, offers his life and love, and gives us entry into his resurrection life.

The church enacts this every year in its supreme liturgy, the Great Vigil of Easter. The congregation gathers in the darkness of the evening before Easter outside the church. A large fire is ignited. From it the sizable paschal candle is lighted, and a deacon carries it into the dark church, the people following behind. The deacon intones "The light of Christ" three times on increasingly higher tones, and the people reply with "Thanks be to God." Each congregant is given an individual candle that is in turn lighted from the great paschal candle. Soon the building is filled with light. People have become a community. Much else follows in this extraordinary liturgy, but the point has been made. In Christ we have moved from darkness to light, from loneliness to community, from silence to praise. Later in the Great Vigil will come baptisms and the first eucharist of Easter. It will become an experience of the paschal mystery. Liturgy helps us practice for life. What happens in the Great Vigil can happen in us. From error to truth, from darkness to light, from death to life, that is the paschal mystery into which the sacraments initiate us and from which we live in Christ. And it changes everything.

Summary: By the sacraments we share in the dying and rising of Christ.

Discussion question: In the sacraments the Risen Christ encounters us and acts on us in order to bless us and make us his own. How does that make you feel? What changes does it evoke for the way you view your life?

Action item: Develop a list of words to describe your response to the paschal mystery.

3

The Necessity of Complexity

No one would claim that humans are simple beings, easy to understand and to explain. For example, my wife and I have been married forty-six years, yet she often remains a mystery to me. I cannot always understand her thoughts or clarify her actions. All us have a veiled and enigmatic quality.

We encounter each other as complex and mysterious beings. Remember, for instance, that we are fully outfitted with dualisms: mind and heart, body and spirit, the physical and the emotional, the conscious and the unconscious, our introverted and extroverted aspects, and the active and the passive. We can hardly make sense of ourselves sometimes.

No human encounter or communication is ever a matter of simple words and straightforward reason. We need actions, signs, symbols, gestures, ritual, and all the arts to convey who we are and to carry the substance of our identities. Some say that eighty per cent of communication is non-verbal.

Think of a couple beginning a love affair. There will be significant words, of course, but some of the best communication takes place without words. Hugs and kisses are exchanged, gifts and tokens given, dinners spent together, and even simply sitting together in silence. In all these ways one human being confronts another, overcoming disparities and differences and making deep connections.

We have said that the Risen One encounters us in two basic and dependable ways, word and sacraments. Recall that Jesus himself is preeminently the Word and the original sacrament, the person who embodies all the complexity of the Holy One. In a secondary way the Holy Bible is God's Word in so far as it points us to Jesus the Word and mediates his presence to us. Christians spend significant amounts of time with the Bible, but that is not an end in itself. Jesus is the point of the Bible, and he stands as the richness of God's mercy and holiness.

The sacraments are no less rich and intricate. In fact, I venture to say that part of the point of the sacraments lies in the fact that they move us beyond mere words and simple logic to the deepest part of our identity and our being. Think of the sacraments as working according to this formula: words + material (bread, wine, water) + action + meanings = encounter.

And consider a sampling of the possible images used to describe sacramental events:

- heaven and earth come together in a close encounter;
- the veil in the Temple is ripped apart so that we have access to the Holy One;
- Christ reaches across time and space to grasp us and bless us;
- we cross the threshold into what the New Testament called the new creation and the kingdom of God;
- the past is made present as we remember Jesus' life, death, and resurrection;
- we are given a glimpse of God's future; and
- people participating in the gospel sacraments are united in ways that transcend time, space, and all human distinctions such as race and nation.

This is only the start of a list. You may well have more to add from your own experience.

The Necessity of Complexity

Furthermore, the materials used in the sacraments—water, bread, and wine—carry multitudes of associations and meanings. Think of water. We know it is necessary for life, and that our bodies are composed largely of it. It cleans. It refreshes. Without it in the desert we can die within a matter of hours. I live a couple of blocks from the Pacific Ocean, and that great body of water evokes both awe and fear for me.

Think of bread. I remember reading about a man captured and imprisoned by the Nazis during World War II. He and his fellow prisoners were put on starvation rations. He said that he did not imagine steak and lobster but rather bread, just bread. It seems to be that basic to us. And remember that the ancient Greeks and Romans imagined wine as a god, such was its importance.

We are complex people. The sacraments are complex experiences. And certainly God is complex. From this set of complexities, let me offer some implications for our lives as disciples of Jesus:

- We should not expect to be able to develop a full and complete understanding of the sacraments. This may distress people who enjoy twenty-five-words-or-less definitions. But little in life is that simple. Mysteries always invite us to deeper depths.

- We can spend a lifetime living in the sacraments. If we find them becoming too routine or even boring, we need to evaluate our level of involvement with what is happening in the sacraments. With baptism and the eucharist there is always more to know, to comprehend, to experience, because they are actually an encounter with the Living Lord.

- In the sacraments we receive the fulness of the Risen Christ. Perhaps you have seen a baptism performed with just a few drops of water, or the eucharist administered with tiny bits of bread. Such actions can trivialize what goes on in a sacrament action. But remember that Christ fed five thousand people and there still remained twelve baskets of leftovers. In baptism and eucharist he does not hold back, but rather gives us the fulness of divine favor, presence, and blessing even with tiny drops of water or bits of bread.

- What happens in the sacraments has eternal significance. They really are matters of spiritual life and death. To participate in them is to be granted entry in the new creation, which is a present reality and also extends into eternity. Therefore, approach these holy moments with reverence and with joy.
- Bring all that you are to the sacraments. We all present a public self, which we hope will make us acceptable to others and perhaps even to God, but we also have a hidden side, aspects of ourselves that we wish to keep secret. For our encounter with Christ in the sacraments to be an authentic event we need to be courageous and give all that we are to God.
- The sacraments are an encounter with the Risen Lord of life and love. Those will be times that change everything about your identity, hopes, values, and meaning. Expect to be changed.

Summary: Complex human beings are encountered by a complex God in complex sacraments in such a way that our lives are blessed in deep and complex ways.

Discussion question: What are some of the associations you have with water, bread, and wine? What do they suggest about God?

Action item: Bake bread or make wine, and then offer them for use in the worship of your church.

4

Begin at the Beginning

YOU REMEMBER HOW THE Wizard of Oz begins. Dorothy has been transported from Kansas to Oz. She wants to know where she is and what has happened to her, but chiefly she needs to know how to go home. Glenda, the good witch, and the munchkins tells her that she has to take up the matter with the great Wizard of Oz who lives in the Emerald City, and that to get there she must follow the yellow brick road. One of the great moments in the movie comes when Dorothy carefully touches her toe to the yellow pavement, taking that first step on her journey to the see the Wizard.

In the sacrament of holy baptism we take that crucially important primary step into the reign of God, into Christ's new creation. It begins our adventure, our pilgrimage into the new world that God is working to establish. We have snapshots of what that reign looks like when we hear the stories of Jesus' ministry: the sick are healed, the captive are set free, the dead live, and the good news of divine mercy is proclaimed for all to hear. Even more, we see it when God in Christ is nailed to the cross in an almost incredible act of loving solidarity with the suffering and anguish of humanity and when God raises Jesus from the dead in a victory of God's deathless love over all that separates us from God, even death itself. In baptism, Jesus opens the door to that new way of living and says to us, "Please come in."

Baptism constitutes our life in Christ. Being a disciple of Jesus is completely a matter of living into and out of our baptism. The old ways of living, the ways characterized by self-concern—"it's all about taking care of ol' number one"—are drowned in the merciful grace of God, and we are transferred from the rule of darkness into the new creation. That suggests that the baptized person is known to God, loved by God, and guided by God.

I think it is no accident that Jesus' himself began his work as Savior and Lord when he was baptized in the Jordan River by John the Baptist. The importance of this event is underscored by the fact that all four gospels narrate the story. Each evangelist brings his or her own slant to their record, but all agree in the important details. Let's consider the fullest account of Jesus' baptism, the one found in Matthew 3:13–17. John has been preaching in the Judean wilderness, saying that God was about to do a new thing and that people need to prepare for that by repentance. Baptism for the Baptist was a washing of repentance, a sign of readiness for God' new world. Jesus appears and asks to be baptized in the Jordan, the little river that snakes its way through the wilderness. John seems to have a sense of Jesus' identity, that Jesus is in his own person the arrival of the new arrangement between God and humanity. John objects, saying that he ought to be baptized by Jesus, who replies simply that his being baptized is the right thing to do. The baptism proceeds, and we arrive at the climax of the story when Jesus comes up from the water. The heavens open, and Jesus sees the Holy Spirit, God's invisible presence, descend on him, and the voice of God proclaims, "This is my Son, the Beloved, with whom I am well pleased." And with that the story ends.

Some remarkable matters surface in this account. Jesus saw it as the right thing to do. In some senses it poses theological issues in that Jesus was already in a perfect relationship with God but insisted that it should happen nevertheless. My reading of this is that it represents Jesus' identifying with us. Baptism is certainly the right thing to do for us, and Jesus in his baptism sets the example and leads the way.

Moreover, in his baptism Jesus is granted the Holy Spirit and is identified as the beloved Son of God. The words spoken by the divine voice have several important echoes from the Old Testament that we need not consider now. It suffices to say that in this event the promises of the Hebrew scriptures have come to fulfillment in Jesus. And with that Jesus is now ready to proceed with his public ministry.

What happened to Jesus in baptism parallels what happens to us. First, note that God is present and functions as the main actor in the event. In baptism it is crucially important to understand that it is an act of God, an act in which God makes promises that change everything about who we are.

Second, note that God says that we are known by God. One of the little side notes about baptism comes with the issue of names. The candidate's name is carefully stated. That becomes the person's so-called Christian name, the name by which God knows you. Consider how important your name is. If I want to get your attention, I call your name. If I know and remember your name that implies a level of intimacy that deepens the relationship. Sometimes names recall status in a family. I am named, for example, after my father, who was, in turn, named after his grandfather and uncle. To be baptized proclaims that God knows us as daughter or son on intimate terms.

Three, God promises to give the baptized person the Holy Spirit, the invisible but real presence of the God revealed in Jesus Christ. Not only are we known by God, but God also chooses to dwell in us and with us. That means, in turn, that we are empowered by the divine presence to be agents and ambassadors of Jesus Christ. We have what it takes! We are known, loved, and empowered by God through God's act in Holy Baptism! Have you ever heard better news?

On my desk stands a small icon of St. Cuthbert, the great Celtic saint of the seventh century. He was a monk, a hermit, and a bishop who lived among the people of northern England and southern Scotland, his home base being Lindisfarne, Holy Isle, off the Coast of England in the North Sea. He eschewed riding a horse, preferring to walk so that he could converse with the people he met on the way. When he encountered someone his first question was, "Have you been baptized?" Imagine where that question might lead in conversations today. The question he posed represents how important baptism is. It is the place where we begin in a journey with Jesus Christ. It is the act that changes our identity and the way we view the life and the world. Cuthbert's is the crucial question.

Summary: In baptism God acts on us and initiates our life in Christ as daughters and sons of God.

Discussion question: What images come to mind when you think about baptism? What thoughts and feelings do they evoke?

Action item: If you have your baptismal certificate, look at it and carefully consider what it says.

5

Push the Pause Button

WE HAVE COME TO a place where we should push the pause button. We have been moving along in our discussion of the sacraments. We have noted that they constitute an encounter with the Risen Christ, and that they consist of a combination of acts, interpretive words, and earthly matter all carried out at the command of Jesus himself. And we have said that in this personal encounter the Risen One seeks to bless us with divine grace and presence. These are done in the context of the community, the church, that has been constituted by the Risen Lord through word and sacrament.

We are now far enough along to state three clarifying factors that form a basic frame for understanding and living into the sacraments. First, a primary theological principle is at work here: God uses means. While there are a few, exceptional cases where people have a direct encounter with God, most of us most of the time find God through means. Moses was one of those rare people: "With him I speak face to face—clearly, not in riddles; and he beholds the form of the LORD" (Num 12:8). The rest of us should expect that God will work through agents. I had a doctor who had this slogan on his office wall: God heals, doctors treat. He understood that he was an agent of God, a means of healing. God uses means, and that is God's normal way of acting.

Second, human beings operate with a fair degree of free will. It is not absolute, of course; I cannot choose, for example, to be in two places at once, but I can choose where to be in the present moment. In our discussion this suggests that God may seek us out in many ways, but we have the ability to accept or refuse or simply ignore those divine promptings. Indeed, I suspect most of us frequently find ways to ignore or reject God unintentionally. For instance, we are not quiet or mindful enough to hear God even in something as simple as reading the Bible; we gloss through it and then quickly go on. So, it is quite possible to be baptized, but then live as if we are not. As far as God is concerned, we are known and loved forever, but we are free to live without recognition of that stunning reality.

Three, we can, however, respond positively. And that we call faith. In scripture faith is not basically subscribing to certain doctrines, but is rather a reliance on, trust in, and commitment to God. Jesus says, "I will show you what someone is like who comes to me, hears my words, and acts on them. That one is like a man building a house, who dug deeply and laid the foundation on rock" (Luke 6:47–48). That faith, that trust, lies in that man's certainty that the rock will be firm. Faith receives and holds firmly to the grace of God. This looks like the attitude that relies on and assumes to be true what the sacraments convey to us, namely, the reliable presence and mercy of Christ. Baptism, for example, washes away the barriers between God and human beings. This, in turn, relies on Jesus' revelation of God's reliable and active love. Baptismal living, then, exemplifies gratitude, a desire to seek God, and a deepened intention to love and serve both God and neighbor.

Finally, allow me a side-bar comment. We are a society fascinated by magic. I do not mean tricks or sleights of hand that amaze us but which we know have a logical explanation. I refer to the magic that appears in certain parts of our culture. It is the belief that if you use the right words and rituals you can manipulate spiritual powers. We come across this in some TV shows but also in people interested in such activities as Wicca and satanism. The problem for us lies with the possible misunderstanding that the sacraments represent a sort of church-based magic. So, a properly done and valid baptism might be interpreted as an automatic, free pass into heaven with no regard to the life of the baptized person. Hitler, after all, was baptized.

The sacraments do not function as magic. They find their basis in God's desire to bless us and be in relationship with us and in Jesus' command and promise. They are Christ-centered, and even a cursory look at the gospels show us that Jesus was not subject to manipulation. Moreover, the sacraments function in the context of human freedom, the right and privilege to accept or reject the action of God. The promise of God and the response of faith form the ground in which sacramental living grows.

I used to work at an adjunct instructor of scripture at a local university. I was fascinated by the way some students would soak up the lectures, discussions, and readings like a sponge absorbs water. Others appeared to be completely immune to any aspect of the class. I remember one young man who hid ear buds and the wire to a radio in his long hair; that was his choice, of course, but he was wasting his time and his parent's money. It is no less true of how we deal with God's grace and the sacraments.

Summary: God uses means, humanshave freedom in regard to God, and faith serves as the response to God's actions in our lives.

Discussion question: Give instances of the ways faith in Christ serve as a foundation in your life.

Action item: Plan an appropriate way to celebrate the anniversary of a loved one's baptism.

6

Soaked in Scripture

WATER FUNCTIONS AS ONE of the major characters in the Bible. Consider the following examples.

First, at the very beginning of the biblical story we find primordial water. "The earth was a formless void and darkness covered the face of the deep, while a wind from God swept over the face of the waters" (Gen. 1:2). This verse portrays a dark ocean with winds whipping up great waves. It is the very picture of chaos, a storm at sea in the depth of the night.

Second, in Genesis 6—8 we find the story of Noah and the great flood. Noah, his family, and representatives of the animal world are saved from drowning even as wickedness is washed away in the deluge.

Third, in the major story of the Old Testament we again deal with water. The events are described in the fourteenth chapter of Exodus. The people of God have finally escaped slavery in Egypt through divine intervention, and now they hurry past the borders of Egypt making a mad dash for home. But then they find themselves on the shore of the Red Sea. Behind them are the troops Pharaoh has dispatched to bring them back and in front lay the chaotic waves and wind of the ocean. At God's command, Moses extends his staff over the water and a strong wind blows the waters apart, thus forming a path through the water. The people rush to the far shore while the wheels of the pursuing chariots are trapped in the mud. Since the days of the early church Christians have seen this as a typology for baptism: through water God acts to rescue us.

Fourth, as the now-freed people of God make their way home across the wilderness of Sinai they run out of water, and they raise a great cry of complaint to Moses. Again, God lays out an action plan for Moses. God tell him to take his staff and strike a certain rock. Moses does that, and it releases a stream of water from the rock (Exod 17:1–7). Paul will later make a typological connection between this event and participating in the eucharist. Our ancestors in faith "drank from the spiritual rock that followed them, and the rock was Christ" (1 Cor 10:4).

Let me make a side comment about a word I have used twice, typology. This refers to an ancient way of interpreting scripture. It finds an imaginative connection between one element in a biblical story with an element in another story. This may trouble our sense of history, but it was assumed by the biblical writers that God was at work in all these events, and, therefore, one was free to link stories in this way. It may not be the way we think, but we must acknowledge that some of the writers of the Bible used it. For example, the whole book of Hebrews uses this approach.

Fifth, think about the wonderful story of Naaman, the commander of the armies of Aram, today's Syria. He was plagued with leprosy and heard that a prophet in Israel might be able to cure him. He sets off with gifts for this person, the prophet Elisha, often called simply "the man of God." Elisha tells Naaman to wash seven times in the Jordon River. Naaman is offended. He had expected a great show of incantations and rituals. Furthermore, he wondered why he had to go to the Jordon when Aram had superior rivers. Nevertheless, he was persuaded to wash, and he was cured of his skin disease (2 Kgs 5). Cleansed by water—doesn't this sound familiar?

Sixth, John's gospel makes use of water at several points. In chapter two we find the famous story of Jesus changing water into wine at a wedding feast in Cana (John 2:1–11). In chapter four Jesus meets a Samaritan woman at Jacob's well in the town of Sychar. He declares that he is the living water. In the next chapter Jesus cures the man lame for thirty-eight years at the pool of water called

Bethzatha (John 5:1–9). Here we discover links between Jesus, water, abundant life, and healing. Finally, as Jesus hangs dead on the cross one of the Roman soldiers pierces his side, out of which flow blood and water (John 19:34).

Finally, the Bible opens with water and closes with it. The final vision in the Revelation of John pictures a world transformed by God. There is now a new Jerusalem and a new earth and flowing through the middle of the city is a river, the source of which is the throne of God and the Lamb (that is, the Risen Christ). Beside the river grow the trees of life, the leaves of which are for the healing of the nations (Rev 22:1–2).

These, along with the accounts of Jesus' baptism, constitute the major "water" stories in the Bible. In light of Jesus we can see in all of them reflections of baptism and eucharist. Liturgy reflects this, too. Since in third century, baptismal liturgies have referenced the biblical stories of water as part of the prayer consecrating the water to be used in baptism. These prayers make allusion to many of these stories, and then go on to note the symbolism of water in baptism itself, and finally they conclude by invoking the Spirit on the water that it may be a means of forgiveness and new birth for the person being baptized.

Now we reach the point at which I have been aiming. Through baptism and eucharist we become part of the grand sweep of the story of salvation. The spiritual asks the question "Were you there?" And we answer: we were and we are. The Bible's story has become our story. We have found our place in the unfolding of the divine plan of salvation for the whole cosmos. The sacraments play a primary role in making that possible.

In 1977 the nation was fixed to the television as a mini-series unfolded the story of the family of a slave named Kunta Kinte. It presented in fictional form the family story of Alex Haley, the author of both the book and the series based on it. It also represented part of the story of America by portraying the roots of slavery and racism. It was one of the highest-rated TV series of all time. It set off something deep in the country and sparked for many a pursuit of their own roots, accompanied by a sense that our family story shapes us in important ways. Our roots matter.

Thus, the sacraments make us a part of God's story and of the story of God's people. This has enormous value for us, especially in our rootless and transient culture. In baptism we are joined to Christ, who is the fulfillment of scripture, and we are made part of his mystical body, the church. In Paul's language we are grafted to the tree of salvation when we are "in Christ" in baptism (Rom 11:17). And in the eucharist we share in the family meal that sustains us as members of the people of God through Christ.

Here are salient points:

- We know that we are part of a glorious family. We are not rootless people but have a noble family as the daughters and sons of God and as sisters and brothers of the Lord Jesus.
- We know we belong. Is that not one of our deepest longings, to be part of something bigger than we are, something with a grand purpose?
- This shapes who we are and how we live. I grew up in a small town surrounded by lots of relatives. At family dinners I learned the stories of the family. I developed a sense of my identity from these experiences and I knew that being part of my family had certain expectations associated with it. The same is true and more so when we are part of God's family.
- The sacraments assure us that from God's point of view our being part of God's family is irrevocable and eternal. God will not cast us aside and will not disown us. Of course, we may choose to reject this and live as if we are "on our own," but God will not change God's mind on this matter.

This is who we are. This is where we belong. We can count on it.

Summary: By virtue of God's action in the sacraments we are made part of the grand sweep of the story of salvation and are part of God's family, the church.

Discussion question: Our family story is defined by scripture. What Bible character or story is your favorite, and how does it help define you?

Action item: What person in your story most helped you live into your baptism? Write a paragraph about that person, naming ways that they helped you on the Jesus way.

7

Let's Begin Again

I served as a parish priest for over thirty years. During that time many couples who had been previously married and divorced approached me about officiating at their wedding. A life-long union represents the norm for Christian marriage, but we know that for some this does not always work even with their best efforts and intentions. My observation is that many second marriages succeed. It is as if the couple had said, "Let's begin again with this marriage business."

Who of us has not reached a place where we sense a need to make a new start, to try again, to reset our lives? That might happen in regard to a job, friendships, or a place to live. But sometimes that ache to begin again comes from deep within us. How can I set out in a better direction in life? Where can I find meaning and freedom? How can I be set free from the chains of a painful past?

And it is not just a matter of individuals. Churches, organization, even whole nations reach this point. As I write this country is gripped by a pandemic and by an agonizing awareness of racial and social inequities. All around we see a longing for a new beginning. People are demonstrating in the streets for a re-set for the nation.

Jesus once had a night-time visit with one of the leaders of the Jewish nation, a man named Nicodemus. Here Jesus presses the issue on his visitor. "No one can see the kingdom of God without being born from above" (John 3:3). The last two words in this quote often have another translation: born anew or born again. I suspect Nicodemus must have sat up straight at this mention of the kingdom of God. Many people at that time and place were looking for a fresh start for their nation and their lives. They wanted freedom from Roman occupation and a chance to set the course of their own lives. Moreover, they understood that such a development would be an act of God. Here is Jesus saying that being born from above and being born anew provided entry into God's new reality.

In what follows Jesus and Nicodemus seem to talk past each other at times. I suspect Nicodemus was thinking in terms of political power while Jesus was talking about a new community, a new reality, and a new way to live.

For our purposes Jesus provides two salient points. First, the main ingredient in this new start will be love. And Jesus serves as God's demonstration project of love. "God so loved the world that he gave his only Son, so that everyone who believes in him may not perish but have eternal life" (John 3:16). Note first that love in scripture is not primarily a feeling, but an attitude and way of acting. It consists of putting aside self-concern so as to serve the needs of others. Think of Jesus' parable of the Good Samaritan, for example. Jesus' way is marked with sacrificial love. Also note that the way one enters the new reality, the manner in which we are born from above consists of birth by water and Spirit. "Very truly, I tell you, no one can enter the kingdom of God without being born of water and Spiri" (John 3:5). Spirit refers to God's active yet invisible presence mediated through the water of baptism. This marks our entry into the new community of God's sovereignty, the new creation characterized by love, the new beginning for humanity.

My wife and I moved to Los Angeles several years ago, and that meant, in part, the purchase of a new home. We had an excellent real estate agent, and she showed us many attractive homes and condos. But one particular house caught our attention, and part of the appeal was the remarkable front door, almost a piece of art. "Nice" we said to each other as we entered. That door led into the house that became our home.

Baptism is the entry into God's new beginnings. God's presence, the Holy Spirit, the spirit of the Risen Christ, constitutes the divine power that makes it all happen, a power active in baptism. And it opens for us the possibility of new life, new beginnings, freedom from a painful past. It allows entry into what John's gospel calls "abundant life" or "life to the full" (John 10:10). Life as God's intends it. Life lived well. Life as love. Who would not want that?

But this does not represent a once-in-a-lifetime arrangement with God. The door always stands open. We are always welcome. When we fall out of baptismal living, when we leave the dimension of the life from above, the baptismal door remains open. We can reclaim baptism and it can reclaim us. Who of us does not need a second chance?

Baptism is the gospel in action. And it changes everything.

Summary: We have entry into God's new creation by being born from above through baptism and the power of the Risen Christ.

Discussion question: How does being baptized change the way you perceive yourself, your future, and our world?

Action item: Read John 3:1–18. How are baptism and faith brought together in this passage?

8

Not OK

Would you agree that "Amazing Grace" is a hymn nearly everyone loves? I am always surprised when even apparently nonreligious people sing it with gusto. It was written by John Newton, a British slave trader who had a profound conversion experience. Look at the first stanza:

> Amazing grace! How sweet the sound,
> That saved a wretch like me!
> I once was lost, but now am found,
> Was blind but now I see.

Later, Newton lays out a wonderful, poetic definition of grace:

> The Lord has promised good to me,
> His word my hope secures;
> He will my shield and portion be
> As long as life endures. (*The Hymnal 1982*, number 671)

God has promised life-long blessing, a hope rooted in the promises found in the Bible.

The definition of grace I learned in Sunday School is simpler: it is God's favor, unearned and unmerited. God constantly chooses to bless us, even though we have done nothing exceptional to earn it. Indeed, we sometimes shun God and the blessings God endeavors to give us.

Not OK

God's gracious character comes face to face with our human situation. I know that I am sometimes an OK person, but I also know that sometimes I am clearly not OK. Perhaps I do something good. For example, I collect a bag full of canned goods for my church's feeding program. That suggests I am OK, and that would be true. But I might do that act, not out of pure charity, but also for the warm feeling it gives me and for the praise I receive from the people at church. That is not OK. As we said earlier, we are complicated people.

Given this, if God is going to do good to me, then God is going to need to cut me a considerable degree of slack. That makes for a situation most of us do not enjoy. I myself would like to think I am self-sufficient and independent, so that you don't need to do me any favors. And then we would like to think that we are basically OK, that the non-OK acts are just occasional slips or haphazard lapses in judgment. We live in a self-help culture that affirms that we by ourselves are capable of doing almost anything, except, of course, ridding ourselves of our need to put ourselves first. But with a bit of courage and honesty we can admit the truth about ourselves, that we do not consistently act out of love for God and neighbor.

This non-OKness haunts our lives. It seems to creep into every crack and crevice. The fancy theological word for this situation is sin. It refers simply to our persistent tendency to put self before anyone or anything else. In the most frequently used prayer of confession in my church, we say out loud that our sin is demonstrated in thought, word, and deed, in what we have done, and in what we have left undone, and that the root of it all is that we have not loved God with our whole heart nor our neighbors as ourselves (Book of Common Prayer, p. 360). No one finds this easy to swallow, but I think there exists no way to deny its truth.

When we speak of grace, we are saying that God chooses to bless us, despite our sin, our not-OKness. And Jesus' life, death, and resurrection boldly stand as God's act of grace and mercy toward us.

Two of the most basic and deep needs of our lives are forgiveness and love. We need some way to free ourselves from bondage to guilt and to the sense that we have hurt God, others, ourselves, and even creation itself. Guilt can and does debilitate people. And who does not need the sense that they are loved? All of us desperately desire the sense that we are known, valued, and accepted. Without that life seems futile.

But God acts toward us with grace. That represents how God chooses to deal with us. But how? How is that favor, that blessings, that mercy given to us at a deep level? The sacraments function as God's means of grace, as a primary way God gives us blessing, favor, even God's own presence. So, that sacraments are the good news in action, good news that change everything.

In baptism God reaches out and makes us God's own, no matter what we may have done. On the most basic level the water of baptism suggests the washing away of sins. Or consider the famous sermon delivered by St. Peter on Pentecost. After he has finished people ask what they should do in response to his proclamation of how Jesus' death and resurrection fulfill scriptural prophecies. "'Repent and be baptized every one of you in the name of Jesus Christ so that you may be forgiven'" (Acts 2:38). Or think of the Nicene Creed in which Christians "acknowledge one baptism for the forgiveness of sins."

The eucharist, too, grants us the forgiveness of God. In essence it functions as a renewal of the relationship between God and us established in baptism, and thereby assures us again and again of the steadfast acceptance of God. For many years I used the example of the family meal as a way to prepare children to receive their first communion. I asked that they image supper at their home, and what happens when they are offered food even when they have been naughty. They always understood the story. In a similar way at the church's holy meal the giving of food becomes an act of forgiveness, a sign that we are accepted, that we belong no matter what.

Part of every eucharistic prayer includes the recitation of the words Jesus spoke over the bread and cup at the Last Supper. Over the cup Jesus said, "Drink form it, all of you; for this is my blood of the covenant, which is poured out for many for the forgiveness of sins" (Matt 26:27–28). Every celebration of the Lord's Supper marks a new beginning, a relationship restored, liberation granted, sin forgiven.

Our word "sacrament" comes from the Latin term *sacramentum*, meaning an oath. The sacraments function as God's promise of grace. God has determined always to act out of mercy, always to bless. We are haunted by what we have done, the damage we have inflicted, the disappointment we have wrought. But greater than all this stands God's oath. "The Lord has promised good to me." That is the basic fact of life. And it changes everything.

Summary: Baptism and eucharist convey to us God's forgiveness of sin.

Discussion question: Think of all the instances of grace in your life story.

Action item: Cross yourself. Put fingers on your forehead, the top of the stomach, left shoulder, and right shoulder. This is a reminder of baptism, and always serves as a way to remember your status as a forgiven child of God.

9

The Body

Would it surprise you to know that we are the eyes and ears, the hands and feet of the Risen Lord Jesus Christ in the world today? How would you feel to learn that Christ does his work today through you? Would that not be both an honor and a privilege? That is what we mean when we say that the church is the body of Christ.

If we want to know where such a stunning idea comes from we must turn to St. Paul, the first great theologian of the church. He did not sit down and write a complete theology of the Christian faith, but rather he functioned as a bishop-theologian who had to address issues that arose in the churches under his aegis. In some ways his writing comes across as quite complex, but in truth it grows from a straightforward proclamation: Christ's death and resurrection. To the problems in his churches Paul applies this basic gospel message like salve on a wound. For Paul Christ, the crucified and risen one, always, always stands at the heart of everything.

The church in the Greek port city of Corinth represents one of his most troublesome congregations. They wrestle with many issues, the most basic being divisions based on spiritual arrogance. In order to combat this condition he develops the concept of the church as the body of Christ. He carefully notes that the body consists of a single unit with many parts or members, each having an

The Body

important role to play. All parts work for the good of the body. If one part suffers, all suffer. And the body is governed by the head. And then he arrives at the punch line: "Now you are the body of Christ and individually members of it" (1 Cor 12:27). He then lays out a sample list of the parts of the body: apostles and teachers, people with gifts of healing and of doing powerfully good deeds, administrators and leaders. And all are under the headship of Jesus.

I have given a quick summary. Paul has more to say in both the passage above and in Romans. I find it impossible to think that Paul is using a metaphor, the church is *like* the body of Christ. I believe he meant it in an ontological sense: we *are* the Body of Christ here and now.

And each Christian has skills, interests, and experiences that allow them to use those in the service of Christ. Each church, too, has its own gifts and skills to function as a part of the body. For example, I was for many years a priest of the Diocese of West Virginia. The motto of that great body is "For Christ and the Church." That accurately states how things work in the Body; we serve our Lord in and through the church.

We have, then, the great privilege and high honor of being a part of nothing less than the Body of Christ. This gives us the sense of being valued and of being engaged in a meaningful life, which are qualities for which we deeply long and without which we fail to thrive.

Now we arrive at the major point in this chapter. We are made part of the body of Christ via baptism. "For just as the body is one and has many members, and all the members of the body, though many, are one body, so it is with Christ. In the one Spirit we were all baptized into one body . . . and were all made to drink of one Spirit" (1 Cor 12:12–13). Once again we see the Risen Christ acting in and through the sacrament of baptism, in this case incorporating us into his own self in such a way that we become his members.

What might happen to us if we were to incorporate this as part of our basic identity? What difference would it make to us and to all whom we contact?

The story of Paul's conversion surely provides one of the most dramatic events in the New Testament. Paul had been an ardent adherent to his Jewish faith, and, indeed, seems to understand Christians as heretical members of the faith. He set about to find Christians, and to bring them under discipline, which could include capital punishment. He received permission from the religious leaders in Jerusalem to go to the synagogues in Damascus, rout out followers of Jesus, and bring them in chains back to Jerusalem for punishment. On the way to that city a flash of light from heaven enveloped him and he fell from his horse. Listen carefully to the first words spoken to him by a voice: "Why do you persecute me?" Paul asks for the identity of the speaker. The reply was: "I am Jesus, whom you are persecuting" (Acts 9:4–5). Paul was told to go into the city and there he would be told what to do. He got up but was unable to see. During the following three days he was blind and did not eat. A local Christian named Ananias had a vision from Christ in which he was told to seek out Paul, lay hands on him, and heal him. And Ananias did as instructed, even though he knew about Paul's reputation as a persecutor. After hands had been laid on Paul he could see again, and the very next thing he did was to be baptized.

I think that the experiential roots of Paul's theology of the body of Christ lay in this event, the great turning point in his life. He learned that to persecute Christians was to persecute Jesus himself.

Body and baptism, note the connection. By virtue of baptism we have the enormous honor and awesome responsibility to live as the Body of Christ. We really are the hands and feet, eyes and ears of our Savior.

Summary: In baptism we are made part of the body of Christ and thus become participants in Christ's mission in the world.

Discussion question: What does it feel like to be part of God's grand plan of salvation? Does it change the way you think about yourself and your church?

Action item: Design a body of Christ/baptism badge that could be worn as a family crest.

10

The Best Gift of All

DOES ANYONE ELSE THINK of their spouse as a wonderful gift from God? I certainly do. Forty-six years ago at St. Paul's Church in Glenside, Pennsylvania, we were united in marriage and our relationship stands as a great blessing to me still.

In baptism we are initiated into a wonderful relationship with Christ. In the New Testament baptism happens by water and the Holy Spirit. Those two factors always go together. Water serves as the outward agent of the workings of the Holy Spirit. Think again of the episode in which Jesus has a night-time meeting with Nicodemus, one of the religious leaders of Jerusalem. Jesus tells Nicodemus that in order to enter the Kingdom of God one needs to be born into this new reality via water and the Spirit (John 3:5).

Let's clarify this a bit. When we speak of the Holy Spirit we are pointing to an invisible yet genuine reality. The danger we face with the word "spirit" lies with our tendency to think of it as something ethereal, a creature of mind and imagination but certainly not real. The fact that the King James Bible translates it as "Holy Ghost" only makes it worse. For the Bible, however, it denotes a genuine reality, which simply happens to exist beyond our senses. It is noncorporeal yet authentic.

Moreover, I find it helpful to remember that the Risen Christ is, in fact, the Spirit. I know this does not represent a full, trinitarian description, but it is biblical (2 Cor 3:17) and helps connect us with Jesus and our baptism. Classical theology states that all of who Jesus was continues in the Risen Lord. For example, when the Risen One encounters his followers on the evening of the first Easter he shows them the wounds in his hands and side (John 20:20). The Jesus of the manger, the cross, and the empty tomb is the eternal, death-conquering, life-bestowing Risen Lord. Invisible yet real he is given us in baptism. He dwells in us, and thereby we become part of the new creation, the Reign of God, of which he remains the constituent reality.

You may sense, then, that baptism represents an initiation rite, and, indeed, it is often referred to in just those terms. Most groups have some sort of ritual by which people are made members. Sometimes it can be simple. When I joined Kiwanis, for example, I signed some papers and then stood before the gathered club to be welcomed. To become part of the home-owners club you need the guidance of a real estate expert to help you deal with scores of forms to be signed and notarized and checks to be written. Every living organization needs an initiation, just as every country needs a boundary and every organism needs some kind of outer membrane or skin. A group with no formal initiation would suggest that there exists no established group, and any group without initiation risks losing both its identity and life. Baptism serves as the crucial initiation into Christ and Christ's church.

So, God gives us Jesus, the Risen One, in and through the sacrament of baptism. It stands as the gift of a new relationship, a permanent relationship. Baptism, then, asks us to trust two realities. First, trust that the Risen Christ will be present in our lives working the ways of his deathless love. Second, trust that fact until the end of time. The relationship Christ establishes with us in baptism is perpetual, enduring, eternal, and immutable. Baptism declares to us: you can always count on Jesus, through thick and thin and even death.

When I was about ten my parents began the process of building a new house, and I was fascinated by it all. The bulldozer came first and dug a great hole. The next evening my dad and I went to visit the site, and I saw that someone had dug a trench around the bottom of the hole and had filled it with cement. "What is that?" I asked. "That's the foundation," replied my dad. "It holds up the whole house." I thought to myself, "It had better be strong." Through baptism we have a rock solid relationship with the Jesus the Risen Lord. Furthermore he is strong. He even conquered death.

From this we can draw five conclusions.

- Because of baptism we know where we stand in life. We have learned that we are firmly anchored on Jesus, the very image of our merciful God.
- We know to whom we belong. As human beings we always belong somewhere, we always are serving someone or something. Via baptism we know we belong to Christ. He loves us and we love him.
- We know the future will be OK, even if we do not know the details. If Jesus is our rock—and baptism affirms that to be true for us—then the storms can rage and the winds can blow but we will come through it.
- We know that Jesus desires a profound relationship with us. Baptism stands as the invitation to enter into a transformational relationship based on divine compassion.
- We know that we can respond with baptismal living. I think it is important to speak of the Christian life as baptismal in nature. It roots our relationship with Christ in a time-and-space event that continually calls us back to Jesus himself. In this way it centers us in the right place. Of course, we can choose to ignore both Jesus and our baptism, but that in no way negates the fact that we belong to him.

In some churches the act of baptism is followed by certain ritual actions that serve as demonstrations of what has happened in the baptism itself. One of these actions uses chrism, oil consecrated by the bishop as a sign of baptismal grace. The priest or bishop puts the chrism on the thumb of his or her right hand, and with it inscribes a cross on the forehead of the newly baptized. The interpretive words accompanying the action are these: you are sealed by the

Holy Spirit in baptism and marked as Christ's own forever. I think the appropriate response to that declaration would be: WOW.

Summary: In baptism we are initiated into a permanent and reliable relationship with Jesus Christ.

Discussion question: How might the fact of your baptism change the way you face a crisis?

Action item: This permanent relationship can be termed a covenant. Write out the terms of a baptismal covenant as you understand it.

11

The God We Fear

WE MIGHT WANT TO deny it. We are likely offended by the idea of it, but far back in the dark corners of our minds, we fear God. Think about it. Feel your way down into the deep parts of your heart. Is it not true that we feel anxious in the presence of the Holy One? Indeed, the idea of God's holiness suggests that a measure of fear may represent a proper response. To say that God is holy is to posit that God is perfect, without fault, and always acts with perfect integrity. That in itself should give us pause. I remember the beginning of a sermon by my Old Testament professor in daily chapel at seminary. He said, "If you think of God as your friend, you are in deep trouble."

In 1917 a German theologian named Rudolf Otto published a book entitled *The Idea of the Holy*. It created a stir and is, in fact, still in print today. Otto's contention is that when we have an experience of the divine we have two responses, which he called *tremedum et fascinan*. That is, when we encounter God we are both terrified and fascinated.

I once had a religion professor as a member of a congregation I served. He decided to test Otto's thesis, and he did so by interviewing many people. He said that nearly everyone identified an experience of the divine and that these were accompanied by fear and fascination.

The Bible itself records such incidents. Remember when God encountered Moses in the burning bush. God instructed Moses to remove his sandals, because he was standing on holy ground. And then God identified God's self: "'I am the God of your father, the God of Abraham, the God of Isaac, and the God of Jacob.' And Moses hid his face because he was afraid to look at God" (Ex 3:6). And then recall God's meeting with the prophet Isaiah in the Temple. The prophet catches a glimpse of God sitting on a throne. And he exclaims, "Woe is me! I am lost, for I am a man of unclean lips, and I live among a people of unclean lips" (Isa 6:5). And think of the story of Peter fishing all night but catching nothing. Jesus tells him to go to deep water and let down the nets with the result that he caught so many fish that the nets began to rip and the boat began to sink. In that moment Peter has an insight into Jesus' identity. He falls to his knees and says, "Go away from me, Lord, for I am a sinful man!" (Luke 5:8).

I hope I have convinced you of what I suspect you already sense, that God is holy and that when we stand before God we kneel in fear and fascination. That functions as a basic and legitimate experience of God, and we should acknowledge it.

Then we come to the waters of baptism. It serves as a solemn pledge from God, a pledge that God will bless and value us. In baptism the heavens are ripped open, and the divine voice says to us, "I embrace you, I bless you, I will treat you with mercy, I am delighted with you, and I will go the limit to grasp you with my love." God may be holy, but God also is love.

And God promises to treat us with grace and mercy. This stands as a universal and eternal promise.

The writer of 1 Peter in the New Testament comments on this link between baptism and divine grace. He recalls the story of Noah and the flood, noting that eight people were saved in the ark. And then comes the punch line: "And baptism, which this prefigured, now saves you—not as a removal of dirt from the body, but as an appeal to good conscience, through the resurrection of Jesus Christ" (1 Peter 3:21). The theme of both Noah and baptism lies with God's salvation through water.

Again, recall the concrete nature of biblical religion. It consists of deeds done, blessings made real, prophecy fulfilled. It portrays a God involved with actual people in time and space.

It never consists only of ideas and emotions, but always involved real people and concrete things. The incarnation of Christ represents the epitome of this idea. Given that, the sacraments exactly express God's usual pattern of interaction with us. And they are, as we have said earlier, necessary for the way that we interact with God and others.

One of Jesus' parables pulls together the themes of God's pledge of mercy and of the sacramental and incarnational manner of God's action. I refer, of course, to the story of the prodigal son. The younger of two sons decides the go off on his own in an act of rebellion. He asks for his share of the inheritance, an insulting act of huge proportion, and then he goes far from home and fritters away his money frivolous ways. He ends up doing what no Jewish person would tolerate, tending pigs. He decides to go home, and even practices an apology. But before he even gets home, his father spots him. "But while he was still far off, his father saw him and was filled with compassion; he ran and put his arms around him and kissed him" (Luke 15:20).

As the son begins to stutter out his little speech his father interrupts and tells the servants to bring out a robe for his son and to put a ring on his finger and sandals on his feet, and then the father commands a huge feast to celebrate his son's return.

What would it be like if the story said that the father simply felt compassion, and then ended at that point? The son would know nothing about the forgiveness of his father, and the parable would go nowhere. In order to be a story about the workings of the Reign of God, actions and objects are required. The father hugs and kisses the young man, he gives him new clothes and a ring, and then they have a party that likely went on for days. The love comes through the acts and gifts of the father. So in a similar way God our Father chooses to treat us.

When I was serving as Bishop of Montana one of the prominent laymen of the diocese was chatting with me one day. He had worked as a representative of the Bureau of Land Management in eastern part of the state. It was an odd tale he told. He said that he was often greeted by ranchers and farmers telling his to get off their property, and some even pulled out their rifles as a threat. It reached that place where residents were threatening his family, and that provoked his resignation from the BLM. I said, "I can hardly believe that. That's terrible. And I don't understand it." He replied, "Oh, I understand it. They don't believe anyone loves them."

I then sensed the truth of it. They lived in a harsh climate doing a job that is especially unpredictable. They are usually isolated from other people. No wonder they concluded that life often works against them.

But remember Peter and the catch of fish. Jesus always meets us at the water's edge and tells us to go deeper. Great blessings await us in the water. That's the way God works.

Summary: We need to say that Almighty God is neither safe or comfortable. Bsaptism stands as God's pledge that we are known, valued, and loved.

Discussion question: If you believed that God is active in our lives, and that your baptism is a divine pledge of blessing, how might that change the way you live?

Action item: Go online and find a copy of Rembrandt's print of the Prodigal Son. Contemplate it.

12

Christ's Story, My Story

LET ME OFFER THREE short narratives. First, one of my prime responsibilities when serving as Bishop of Montana was overseeing our summer camp, its staff, and programming. I understood this as crucial because it was a transformational place for most of the attendees; it was a place where they met Jesus. As a result of vigorous programming nearly every year some campers or staff persons asked to be baptized, and that took place in Flathead Lake on whose shore stood the camp. They candidate and the priest would wade out into the crystal clear lake, and as the person was baptized they were entirely placed under the water. Because of the setting and the ample supply of water these events were unlike your average baptism in a small font in a church. The moment of high drama came as the person disappeared under the surface. They had been well and truly baptized.

Second, when I was about six years old my mother decided that I was going to learn to swim at the YMCA. I resisted strongly. I had tested things out in the bathtub and I knew that I did not float. Added to this was the fact that we lived beside the great Ohio River, and I knew something of how dangerous water could be. Drownings, accidental and intentional, were common. I did not intend to die in a swimming pool. I may have resisted, but my mother won the argument, and off to the Y I went. My big discovery came when I realized that I did, in fact, float in water.

Third, I have had the privilege of presiding over many Great Vigils of Easter. This spectacular service stands as the climax of the liturgical year. Let's briefly review it again. It begins in the darkness of the Saturday evening before Easter Sunday. A fire is ignited by the deacon, and the celebrant blesses it, asking that our hearts will burn with heavenly desires as a result of Easter. From this sanctified fire the Paschal candled is lighted, and then deacon carries it into the darkened church with the congregation following. At three points he or she pauses and intones "The light of Christ." The people reply by singing "Thanks be to God." From the Paschal candle each congregant lights a small individual candle, so that they church now glows with light. The deacon then chants a wonderful hymn of praise called The Exultet. Here are a few snippets. "This is the night, when all who believe in Christ are delivered from the gloom of sin, and are restored to grace and holiness of life . . . How holy is this night, when wickedness is put to flight, and sin is washed away." Next follows a series of Old Testament readings, the primary one being the story of the crossing of the Red Sea. The prayer that concludes this reading says in part that the Red Sea story functions as "a sign for us of the salvation of all nations by the water of baptism." After the reading always follows baptisms and the renewal of baptismal vows. And it all ends with a joyful celebration of the first eucharist of Easter (The Book of Common Prayer, pp. 285–295). This service again and again links Christ, the light of Easter, salvation, and baptism.

These incidents pull together baptism and the life and death of Jesus. And they help prepare us to consider perhaps the most profound aspect of baptism: we are joined to the death and resurrection of Jesus through the water of baptism.

The salient biblical passage comes from Paul. "Do you not know that all of us who have been baptized into Christ Jesus were baptized into his death? Therefore we have been buried with him baptism into death, so that, just as Christ was raised from the dead by the glory of God the Father, so we too might walk in newness of life. For if we have been united with him in a death like his, we will certainly be united with him in a resurrection like his" (Rom 6:3–5). Once again, we need to understand that God is acting on us in this sacrament and is altering our reality. From now on, we will share in Christ's story. His story will become our story. That stands as God's pledge made in this solemn event.

As a middle school student I was struck for the first time by what was said and what was not said about Jesus in the Creed. I expected a summary of teachings and commands, but instead I noted a bare bones account of his life: he was born, he died, he was raised, and he will come again. The movement from life to death to new life makes up the story of Jesus. That pattern now becomes the story of the life of baptized persons and of the church itself. God will be active in our lives making life out of death, hope out of despair, and purpose out of meaninglessness.

I certainly do not consider the above Romans passage to be simply a metaphor. I believe it represents the truth that baptism changes us by promising God's presence in our future. It changes us as we stand before God; God sees us a sisters and brothers of Christ, as united to Christ. It changes us as we consider ourselves; we are now part of Christ, intimately joined to him through time and eternity. This is no metaphor but rather an ontological reality.

We can state it simply. As God worked in Jesus' life, so God will work in our lives.

As I write the COVID virus has overtaken the world. Some experts say that it will be with us in the future and only a yet-to-be-developed medicine can confine it. In the meantime all the predictable activities of life have been upended. For example, I have just watched a baseball game in which the only fans present were cardboard cut-outs and all the crowd sounds were recordings. What is more predictable than baseball? And yet even it is radically altered by the pandemic. No wonder we see news reports on TV telling us that fear and anxiety will be more common. Despite this, we know that the virus has merely focused an aspect of normal life; we live in a world largely beyond our control and sometimes beyond our ability to cope. How do we live in such a world?

Perhaps the most frequent refrain in scripture says, "Do not be afraid." In light of the death and resurrection of our Lord and of our baptism into him this phrase takes on new depth.

We can trust that our future will be one of blessings and hope. Even in the midst of tragedy and pain the Risen Lord, the victor over death, is at work bringing light out of the dark. Baptism assures us that our story is Christ's story, that light will come from the darkness for us. What happens might not be what we want, but we can rest with the assurance that God will make something good out of it. The paschal mystery stands as the reality in which we live. Because Christ lives, we shall live. Does that not change everything?

Summary: In baptism we are joined to the death and resurrection of Christ.

Discussion question: The movement from darkness to light typifies life in Christ. Can you think of instances of this in your life? How does this enable you to walk with Jesus through life?

Action item: Handel's "Hallelujah Chorus" is often sung at Christmas, but in fact is from the Easter portion of Messiah. Listen to it again as you remember that you are baptized.

13

Shifting Gears

WE CAN USE ONE particular word to summarize the message of the Bible: covenant. In ordinary usage it suggests a binding agreement, a contract, an important arrangement. We often refer to marriage, for example, as a covenant. In the scriptures, however, the idea of covenant contains a surprising and vital twist. In the Bible God always initiates the covenant and God makes it work. It does not function as a relationship between equal partners, as is the case in marriage. In scripture, God always abides by the covenant.

For instance, the people of Israel have been freed from slavery in Egypt and guided across the wilderness as they head toward home. Along the way they stop at Mt. Sinai. God speaks to Moses, "Thus you shall say to the house of Jacob, and tell the Israelites: You have seen what I did to the Egyptians, and how I bore you on eagles' wings and brought you to myself. Now, therefore, if you obey my voice and keep my covenant, you shall be my treasured possession out of all the peoples. Indeed, the whole earth is mine, but you shall be for me a priestly kingdom and a holy nation" (Exod 19:3–6). What follows are the terms of the covenant, the Ten Commandments. Later the covenant is ratified in blood and with a covenant meal eaten in God's presence (Exod 24). You sense the importance of this covenant forged at Mt. Sinai. God formally adopts the people of Israel and names them as holy, set apart, for God. The covenant finds its basis in God's saving actions to liberate and save the Israelites and in God's promise to be with and protect them in the future. God initiates and remains the primary actor.

We need to say again that in baptism God initiates a covenant with us. We then belong to God forever and God promises to be a blessed presence in our lives always. In baptism, God claims us and promises to work resurrection in and through us. Remember that the very word "sacrament" is based on the Latin term for oath and promise. Baptism, then, initiates us into a covenant of promise and serves as God's oath to us.

Now we shift gears and move on to consider more fully the other great gospel sacrament, eucharist. We tend to give many names to anything we value highly. I have, for example, eight different names for Gemma, my wonderful cocker spaniel. In a similar way this sacrament has many names: the Lord's Supper, Holy Communion, the Mass, the Divine Liturgy, the Holy Mystery, and Holy Eucharist. And each name connotes a different aspect of this sacrament.

Part of both the importance and value of the eucharist lies in the fact that we are involved in it so often. My own church, for instance, mandates its use every Sunday, and many congregations celebrate more often than that. Its frequency, too, tells us something about its worth and benefit.

Because of its frequency and its meaning we come to depend on the eucharist as one of the main pillars of our faith along with scripture and prayer. Our journey with Jesus begins with baptism and is sustained by eucharist, the Bible, and our prayers. As was the case with the Exodus story above we see it as our covenant meal, the setting in which our Lord comes to us and feeds us on his resurrection presence.

On the night of his betrayal Jesus gathered his disciples for a meal. He commanded that they continue the meal: "Do this in remembrance of me." When we disciples gather we share this meal in which we remember the sacrifice of the cross and participate in the resurrection presence of Jesus. Every week begins with this high moment of communion with Christ.

Let's begin our journey of discovery into the meanings and implications of this great sacrament.

14

More Covenant

THE EUCHARIST HAS DEEP roots in the narrative of the Old Testament. As noted earlier probably the major story in the Hebrew Bible is the Exodus. It begins when the descendants of Jacob find themselves enslaved in Egypt. They have prayed for deliverance to the God of their ancestors, and God hears and responds, acting in a way that suggests a covenant relationship. Through Moses God delivers the people from slavery. They escape under cover of darkness, racing east into the desert toward home. They are trapped at the Red Sea, but again God acts and delivers them. They continue their wilderness journey and are led to Mt. Sinai, the mountain of God.

There at the foot of the mountain God begins the process of forging a covenant with all the people of Israel, not just with single persons as was the case with Abraham, Isaac, and Jacob. There and then God speaks through Moses, "Thus you shall say to the house of Jacob, and tell the Israelites: You have seen what I did to the Egyptians, and how I bore you on eagles' wings and brought you to myself. Now therefore, if you obey my voice and keep my covenant, you shall be my treasured possession out of all the peoples. Indeed, the whole earth is mine, but you shall be for me a priestly kingdom and a holy nation. These are the words that you shall speak to the Israelites" (Exod 19:3–6). The people respond, "Everything you have spoken we will do" (Exod 19:8) So the covenant finds its basis in the saving action of God, which the people recognize and acknowledge.

God then prepares for the next stage of the process. The people are to prepare themselves for a special, holy event, and God reveals God's nearer presence with smoke, fire, and thunder from the mountain's summit. Moses ascends the mountain and there receives the basic component of the covenant, the Ten Commandments. Notice especially how they begin: "I am the LORD your God, who brought you out of the land of Egypt, out of the house of slavery; you shall have no other gods before me" (Exod 20:2). Again God provides the basis for a covenant in God's saving action, and then says that the people must have no other gods except the LORD. In one verse we have the heart of the covenant, God's blessing and the people's acknowledgment of that blessing in their lives.

Various twists and turns occur, but we come to the place where the covenant must be formally ratified. We have an account of an especially solemn and serious occasion. First, the leaders of the people build an altar of twelve stones, each representing one of the tribes. Then they offer an ox which is slaughtered and its blood is drained into a basin. Remember that for ancient people blood represented life itself; the ox stands as a substitute for the lives of the people themselves. In effect they are laying their lives before God. Moses takes half of the blood and dashes it on the altar, which represents God, and half on the people. Moses declares, "See the blood of the covenant that the LORD has made with you" (Exod 24:8).

Then comes the second and climactic moment. Moses along with the seventy elders of the people are brought into God's presence at the summit. They see the sapphire-like pavement before God's throne. With some sense of surprise the text says that God did not lay a hand on them. Then comes this astonishing phrase: "Also they beheld God, and they ate and drank." (Exod 24:11).

I have taken the time to reiterate this narrative because of its importance in understanding both covenant and eucharist. Please note these three factors:

- Everything is based on God's initiative, which consists of mighty acts of liberation and salvation. The people of Israel simply would not have existed without God.
- Blood is involved. As stated above, it represents life. It still does. The Red Cross makes its appeal for blood donations under the motto of "Save a Life."
- The eating of a meal in God's presence seals the covenant and stands as a sign of God's continued grace and favor.

With those comments we begin to sense the connection between the Mt. Sinai covenant and the covenant expressed in the eucharist. Again, note three factors.

- Christians always see the life, death, and resurrection of Christ as the summation and climax of God's dealings with us. In Jesus God is, in effect, acting personally in the process—no mediators, no written statements, no prophets, just God in Christ. The death of Jesus demonstrates the depth of God's covenantal commitment, and the resurrection shows God's ability to keep the covenant in any contingency.
- The blood of Christ seals the covenant. This partly consists, of course, of the blood shed on the cross. But remember also Jesus' words over the cup: "This is my blood of the covenant, which is poured out for many for the forgiveness of sins" (Luke 26:28). When we drink from the cup during the eucharist we are imbibing the new covenant God establishes with us through Jesus.
- We stand in God's presence when make our way to the altar to commune. With Moses and the seventy elders we present ourselves to God and catch a glimpse of him present in the eucharist.

When we eat and drink the consecrated bread and wine we put ourselves in the presence of the Risen Christ, and in so doing we are re-ratifying and re-acknowledging the covenant he has made with us in baptism.

The eucharist identifies us as the people of the new covenant, the graceful relationship God has made with us in and through Jesus Christ. It again and again, week-in-and-week-out, assures us of our bond with our merciful savior. But we need to add two more factors to the eucharistic covenant. First, we look at Paul's correspondence with the eucharistic people in Corinth, the great Greek seaport city of the ancient world. Their eucharists have gone awry with the wealthier people coming early and consuming the holy bread and wine, leaving little or nothing for the others who had to work until dark. Paul chides them, "Do you show contempt for the church of God and humiliate those who have nothing?" (1 Cor 11:22). Then he solemnly retells the story of the Last Supper as the basis for what he says next. "Whoever, therefore, eats the bread or drinks the cup of the Lord in an unworthy manner will be answerable for the body and blood of the Lord. Examine yourselves, and only then eat of the bread and drink of the cup" (1 Cor 11:27–28). Paul reminds the Corinthians that the eucharist consists of a divine-human encounter, a matter to be taken with great seriousness. This in part means preparation to receive the Lord in the bread and wine but also consideration of the other members of the Body of Christ who will also commune. For those of us who commune frequently this passage serves as a shocking wake-up call to what we are participating in when we eat and drink during the covenant meal.

Second, I turn to the baptismal covenant liturgy in my church's Book of Common Prayer. As part of being baptized the candidate along with the congregation affirm and re-affirm the covenantal relationship forged in the water of baptism. The first three questions of the Baptismal Covenant have to do with basic belief, which takes the form of repeating the three articles of the Apostle's Creed. Then follow five questions about behavior and lifestyle. The very first asks, "Will you continue in the apostles' teaching and fellowship, in the breaking of bread, and in the prayers?" (BCP, p. 304). The priority of this question expresses rightly the importance of the eucharist as a way of living in covenant with God.

When I was a child we sometimes had Sunday dinner at the home of my grandparents. This was an event to which I looked forward eagerly. My grandmother was a wonderful cook in an old-fashioned, southern way. I am sure she had never heard about fat grams or calories. She just fixed delicious foods, often a roast with mashed potatoes and vegetables. Part of the experience for me was that I as the oldest grandchild got to sit at the "big table" with the adults. It was there that I learned the stories of my family and it was where I felt I belonged. The dinner usually ended with pineapple upside-down cake topped with real whipped cream. Some sixty years later whenever I have that cake I am transported back to my grandparents' kitchen.

This story functions as the personal roots for my experience of eucharist as covenant. I believe the biblical narratives we have considered tell the same story. The eucharist is a covenant meal, a place where the past is brought forward to the present through remembrance, where we recall what it has cost in life-terms to be in a solemn relationship, and when we experience that we are a deeply valued member of God's family. And that naturally means that we are intimately related to the other baptized persons who commune with us, as Paul graphically has reminded us. The eucharist covenant from my point of view makes us related in a way deeper than DNA.

Those childhood Sunday dinners continue to inform my eucharistic piety. Have you noticed how many important events are marked by meals? Think of wedding banquets, birthday celebrations, graduation parties, anniversaries, promotions and many more.

Something deeply human and deeply personal happens in these events. For us these meals celebrate important connections we have. They lift up the covenants, great and small, that fill our lives. You may know that the word "companion" is based two Latin words meaning "with bread." We generally don't eat with just anyone but rather with those we know and value. Meals and covenants go together. Meals both commemorate and make covenants.

As a bishop I was responsible for nearly every aspect of the life of some forty churches. I visited those places at least once per year, and the highlight of that event was celebrating the eucharist and preaching. In my mind, and I suspect in the minds of most of the members, the focus was not so much me as on the altar and the holy actions that took place there. It was the family meal actualizing the covenant between Christ and his church, between bishop and his or her people and clergy, and between members. From the altar at Mt. Sinai to the altar of our church to the altar-throne of God in the next age, the eucharist re-presents the covenant of grace between Jesus and us.

Summary: In the eucharist, we celebrate and live into a covenant of divine grace first established in our baptism.

Discussion question: What important meals in your life can you compare with the eucharist covenant meal?

Action item: Can you write your own short definition of covenant?

15

Remember to Remember

My wife and I sometimes find it necessary to play the Remember Game. Where is my phone? I can't remember where I put it. Where are the car keys? I can't remember where I placed them.

That certainly represents one of the senses in which we make us of the word "remember." It suggests recalling and recollecting a fact or a detail. And sometimes that can be vital. For instance, we absolutely need to remember our address or our phone number.

But in the eucharist we use the word "remember" in another, deeper sense. Please remember that Jesus himself specially told us to remember him every time we participate in the holy meal. "Then he took a loaf of bread, and when he had given thanks, he broke it and gave it to them saying, 'This is my body, which is given for you. Do this in remembrance of me'" (Luke 22:19). We are solemnly charged to remember the events that took place around the table on the night before he was betrayed.

But what exactly are we to remember? We remember that the bread was broken and the wine poured out just as Jesus' body was broken and his blood poured out on the cross. This special sort of remembering links us with both that last meal and with the grim events of the next day. By the act of bringing myself mentally to the last supper and to the cross I become part of those events. And they become part of my personal story.

I have a small icon entitled "The Mystical Supper." It portrays in the traditional manner of icons that last meal of Jesus. In the center of a long table sits Jesus with bread and cup before him and with six apostles to his left and six to his right. The power of the image lies with the fact that the table curves toward the viewer, suggested that we are being pulled into the events of that night. And by remembering, we are.

Second, we remember that the eucharist functions as a covenant with Jesus himself presiding over the re-ratifying of the covenant first established in baptism. There is, in fact, a sense in which Jesus is the covenant, that he acts as God's anointed agent and that we have been made part of him by water and the Spirit. By our eating and drinking we sign on to the covenant again, we renew our commitment, and we repeat our "yes" to our Lord. In doing this we have placed ourselves squarely in the Reign of God and have agreed to serve as agents of the new creation.

An episode from Matthew's gospel (20:20–28) helps us dig more deeply into this aspect of remembrance. Jesus and the apostles were on the last leg of their final journey to Jerusalem, and perhaps the twelve were anticipating that Jesus would enter the capital city and initiate the coup d'etat by which the new golden age would be established. James and John's mother approaches Jesus and asks that when Jesus has become king he make her two sons co-regents. Jesus replies that it is not within his authority to grant that, but then he looks directly at the two brothers and tells them they do not quite understand what they are asking. "Can you drink the cup I am about to drink" he asks. And they readily say they can. "Then, you will drink that cup," he replies. This exchange infuriates the other apostles, probably because they, too, would like to sit at Jesus' right and left hands in his new kingdom. Jesus calls them together. He reminds them that the Gentiles, those who know little about God, like power and authority, but these do not represent the norms of his kingdom. Service and sacrifice are what make for greatness in God's rule. Then comes the punch line. Jesus tells them that he has not come to exercise power but to serve, and the supreme sign lies in offering his life as a ransom for many.

I have taken some time with this episode because it has much to say about being with Jesus in his meal. Can we drink his cup? If we do we will be partners with him in service and sacrifice. These act as key components in his covenant, and we along with James and John are told that we will, indeed, drink from his cup. That, too, is part of remembering. We are there with James and John and with them we see our future as servants of the one who gave his life as a ransom.

Third, when we take part in the eucharist we remember that he is present in this mystical supper as the Risen Lord. For me another gospel episode stands as a powerful paradigm of this aspect of remembrance. We find it in John 21:1–14. The resurrection has occurred and Jesus has made several amazing appearances to his disciples. Seven of them, however, leave Jerusalem and go fishing in the Sea of Galilee. They spend the night fishing but catch nothing. The Risen Jesus was on the shore, but they oddly do not recognize him. He tells them to fish off the other side of the boat, and they then catch a huge haul. In that event, Peter finally senses who stands on the shore. They bring their nets in and find that Jesus has prepared a breakfast for them, bread and fish over a fire. My sense of the story is that they are standing there in stunned silence and amazement even while knowing who greets them. And Jesus then says, "Come and have breakfast" (vs. 12). This meal marks the beginning of a new day, and it is a meal provided by the Risen Lord himself.

Should we not see our eucharists today in the same way? Is this not what we remember? Does this meal not make the beginning of the new day, the day in which resurrection is present and active?

For those who drink the cup and consume the bread the eucharist becomes a time of remembering, of reliving and re-inhabiting the paschal mystery. This meal stands as an event in which time collapses. The past becomes present. The present opens the door to the future. And the present itself becomes more real, more authentic, as we stand before our Risen Lord and Savior.

When my wife and I were married we saved a piece of our wedding cake in our freezer. On our first anniversary we defrosted it and ate it together. We remembered that special day and the covenant established them. We ate. We rejoiced. We looked to the future. And we remembered.

To be a person means to remember. To be a people means to remember. The remembering forms and shapes our identity. It makes the past present and causes us to consider the future. The act of remembering becomes, then, a vital and necessary part of being a human being and being a people.

For the baptized Jesus continues to command us to remember as we eat and drink. In that we recall where God is centered, that is, in Christ. In that we recall where we are centered, that is, in Christ. What could be more important than that?

I recall some eucharists during which things went wildly wrong. I remember the time I accidently tipped over the chalice and all the consecrated wine poured across the white linen cloth on the altar. The altar guild leader wanted to do me bodily harm. Or I recall the time I was administering the bread and sneezed. It blew the wafers all over the chancel. Angry looks abounded that day.

Those are events I remember. But other than reminding me to be careful, they change nothing. But that other kind of remembering changes everything. We eat and drink the holy bread and wine, we re-enter our covenant with Christ, we place ourselves in his service, we experience the past in the present, and we rejoice in the presence of our Savior. Do this in remembrance of me, Jesus says. Yes, Lord. Amen, Lord.

Summary: The eucharist functions as a mystical meal of remembrance during which the past becomes present and we find ourselves in the presence of Jesus.

Discussion question: How does this weekly act of remembrance enrich your walk with Jesus?

Action item: When you next commune note all the acts that are remembered before God during the eucharistic prayer.

16

I Give You Myself

MANY CHURCHES IN ONE way or another teach that the Risen Christ is present in the eucharist. And often the words that are spoken as the consecrated bread and wine are distributed are: The Body of Christ, The Blood of Christ. That suggests a reality happening at the moment we eat and drink the eucharistic elements, does it not?

But before we launch into a discussion of the eucharist, I want to offer this position: Christ continues to be present as the Risen One in many ways. He speaks to us in scripture, for instance. How often have you heard or read a section of the Bible and seemed to be a truth spoken directly to you from the mouth of Jesus? In my experience the more one works with the Bible in a slow and serious way the more often this happens. Indeed, the ancient practice of *lectio divina*, a prayerful approach to reading the Bible, is calculated to assist.

In prayer the Risen Lord not only hears us and reads our hearts but also whispers his prayer for us. I do not mean to suggest that you ought to expect to hear voices, but I do point to times when we simply sense the presence of Jesus with us and in us and we become aware of a thought of feeling that comes from someplace other than ourselves. It, of course, takes some discretion to separate our thoughts from those of Jesus, but as we learn to know him more and more that discretion develops. Moreover, this can happen in any sort of prayer, public prayer, private prayer, silent prayer, meditation. In any case, Jesus makes himself present to us in prayer.

In the community of the baptized he comforts and challenges us. I can recall occasions when I have been at odds with a person and during the Passing of the Peace forgiveness and a new start in that relationship took place. That does not happen apart from the presence of Christ. Or consider official statements that leaders of churches offer to their people. The bishops of my own church have recently issued a serious call for all members to identify the racism in themselves and to eradicate it. In a body where too many would declare that they are racism-free this statement feels to me like a necessary word from Jesus.

In blessings and absolutions Jesus presents himself to us. Blessings usually occur at some special moments and are intended to be taken as words from God, words of grace and favor. Most commonly this happens during a church service. There we hear that we are forgiven and that we are blessed by God. But I have had many occasions when someone would privately ask for a blessing of a prayer book or a cross or even a pet. These can be times of divine presence, too.

Jesus comes near in the poor. Recently my wife and I were walking into church and sleeping under a bush near the building laid a homeless man. Our congregation has an extensive and important ministry to the many unhoused persons in the neighborhood, and I support that. But that morning, that man seemed to be Jesus again saying, "What are you going to do now?" He reminded again that Jesus was a poor person with no home.

We sense Jesus' presence in the people we meet. They can mediate his presence through both words and actions. Think of a time when someone has said or done something that seemed to have the scent of heaven about it. As priest and bishop I have had times too many to count when someone has said something, written a note, or made a gesture that I needed to hear, even when it was something I resisted.

I need to add a final item to the list that often is overlooked. Christ comes near in music and art. I recall a time when I was part of a group that was trying out some new hymns. One mentioned

I Give You Myself

God carrying us on his shoulders as a parent does with a child, and the man next to me burst into tears. Christ present in the words and music made a deep connection in his life. Or think of icons, that ancient form of art that so powerfully pulls us into prayer and into the presence of God.

I hope by now you sense that Christ comes to us, Christ makes himself available to us in many ways and on many occasions. And I have seldom heard anyone doubt the reality of those encounters. So it should not surprise to learn that the church has declared the presence of Jesus in the holy meal. The official language states that Jesus, the Crucified and Risen Lord, is sacramentally present. And this has been the case since the beginning of the church. Think of the story of the road to Emmaus in Luke 24:13–35. Two disciples are walking from Jerusalem to the village of Emmaus on the first Easter day and as they walk they discuss the reports about Jesus dying and being raised. The Risen Lord joins them, but strangely they do not recognize him. He joins them for supper and at the breaking of the bread they recognize that he is present there. So, from the very beginning we can trace the declaration of Christ's real presence in the sacrament of the altar.

At this point a word of clarification about terminology might help. We speak of the bread and wine as being the body and blood of Christ. This, of course, represents a way of witnessing to the assertion that Jesus is there. But I warn against thinking in overly literal terms. We should not envision this as a cannibalistic act. We say that Christ is spiritually present. Remember that we have been saying that when we use that term "spiritual" we are declaring that the Risen Lord is, in fact, present but in a noncorporeal way.

In the eating and drinking Jesus is saying to us, "I truly give myself to you here and now."

Over the centuries Christians have tried to describe the manner in which we can affirm that Jesus draws near in the eucharist. We can make a quick survey of some of these positions.

- One says, "As I eat and drink in remembrance of Jesus, he comes to me in my mind."

- A similar position says, "As I eat and drink with my mouth, Jesus enters into my heart."
- A third approach states, "In the holy meal I lift up my heart and am taken into the heavenly presence of Jesus." You can sense that these represent nuanced yet similar positions.
- Christ is present in and with the consecrated bread and wine. The bread and wine become the medium of divine reality.
- Finally, another position states, "The bread and wine in a mysterious way become the Body and Blood of Christ." This position is called transubstantiation and is associated with the theology of St. Thomas Aquinas. He used categories of philosophy to explain that the outer characteristics of the bread and wine (the "accidents," the taste and appearance) remain the same but the inner reality (the "essence") become the presence of Christ. This may or may not be convincing, but it attempts to provide a method to deal with something that clearly lies beyond our capability to explain. It clearly takes quite seriously the doctrine of the real presence of Christ in the sacrament of the altar.

My own position is that all these have something helpful and edifying for us to consider, but that none are fully adequate to explain the "how" of Christ's presence. I want to value the help each offers to me.

Of all the ways that Christ comes to us, the eucharist holds an especially important place. It pulls together word, action, prayer, the community, and the needs of the world all under the command of Jesus to eat and drink in remembrance of his death and by the power of his resurrection presence. It functions as a climax of our life together with the one into whom we were baptized. What better way to begin the week than to receive Jesus' offering of himself so that he dwells in us and we in him?.

This implies that we need to approach the eucharist with joy, anticipation, preparation, and seriousness. As I stand before the altar of churches and administer these sacred gifts to people I sometimes wonder about the casual attitude that some seem to take. Perhaps I misread what is happening, but a thoughtless, prayerless, inattentive participation seems beyond the pale in light of the divine-human interaction that is taking place. Part of the impetus for this book lies in my desire for people to be captured by the majesty, wonder, and blessing of the two great sacraments and of the covenant they establish and nurture.

The eucharist also points to the centrality of Christ for us. There's a saying out there that goes, "If it ain't about Jesus, it ain't about anything." Our religion is about Jesus Christ, his sacrificial love for us, and our responsive love for him. My favorite line in the Christmas hymn "O come, all ye faithful" is this: "Who would not love thee, loving us so dearly?" (*The Hymnal 1982*, number 83) Indeed! If we love Jesus, and that is the precise language needed, if we love Jesus would not one of the things we most desire and most anticipate be to receive him as he gives us himself in the sacrament?

Allow me two final comments. First, Elizabeth 1 is supposed to have written the following about the eucharist:

> Christ was the word that spake it,
> He took the bread and brake it,
> And what his words did make it,
> That I believe and take it.

She wrote that during a time of intense religious controversy, which included contentious debate the nature of the sacramental presence or non-presence of Christ in the eucharist. For me her poem still suffices.

Second, no matter what we say about the connection between Christ and the elements of the eucharist, the eucharist itself represents a profoundly intimate encounter with the Risen Christ. It changes everything.

Summary: In the eucharist Christ gives us himself.

Discussion question: How does participating in the eucharist help deepen your journey with Jesus? Please give instances.

Action item: Write a short paragraph about what it means to you to affirm that Christ feeds you in his sacred feast.

17

The Secret Revealed

THE CHRISTIANS WHO MAKE up Eastern Orthodoxy call the eucharist "The Holy Mystery." That points us to a good and useful New Testament term, mystery.

I have written elsewhere that this scriptural term should not be seen as someone or something beyond our ability to know. This would be something about which we would say, "I have no idea." Nor should we understand in the sense of a mystery novel. In those the solution to the mystery is not obvious at first, but you know that with some investigation of facts and some good reasoning it will all be worked out, and the mystery will be revealed in the end. This would be something about which we would say, "Give me some more data and time to think and I will figure out the mystery."

In scripture, mystery moves beyond both of the above definitions. It refers to someone or something the depths of which we cannot comprehend even though we are able to grasp something about it. It is profound, but not completely beyond us. People always remain a mystery to us in this sense. We may know them quite well, but the deepest part of them remains veiled from our sight. God is the deepest of mysteries, and yet we are able both to know about God and to relate to God.

In the New Testament the word "mystery" has two aspects. First, it connotes that the past and mysterious workings of God can be revealed. This is one of those wonderful times when scripture turns words inside out. This happens in 1 Corinthians where Paul is describing the final stage in what can be called the process of salvation. The great break-through came in the death and resurrection of Christ, and now all the baptized live with the hope and the expectation that at the end of the age they too will be raised from the grave in the same way as Jesus was. And then the apostle escorts us into the next step. "Listen, I will tell you a mystery! We will not all die, but we will all be changed" (15:51). Then in beautifully poetic language he speaks of the resurrection of the dead to life imperishable and of the defeat of death itself. The mystery is revealed, but we catch only glimpses of it. A mystery, then, stands as the declaration that God has taken radical action in Christ to save humanity.

The second aspect lies in the revealing not only that God chooses to save but also where that salvation is given. Paul's first letter to the Corinthians again serves as an example. He tells the members of the church there, "When I came to you, brothers and sisters, I did not come proclaiming the mystery of God to you in lofty words or wisdom. For I decided to know nothing among you except Jesus Christ, and him crucified" (2:1-2). The locus of salvation is revealed in Jesus Christ. He represents the mystery of God proclaimed as an open secret.

If we are steeped in scripture to use the word "mystery" is very good news, indeed. We know that we are about the enter the new creation where God's blessing and grace are made abundant in Jesus. Remember our discussion of incarnation in chapter one. The point of that key doctrine lies in its revelation that Jesus, God with us, proclaims salvation and is also the means of accomplishing it. God had slowly and carefully been working out the salvation of humanity, but in Jesus all is revealed, the mystery made public, and all becomes clear.

That brings us to the Holy Mystery, the eucharist. It takes only a small theological leap to understand that the eucharist is an event of mystery, a public occasion when salvation is declared and made available for us. Paul, again, says that whenever we celebrate this meal we proclaim the death and resurrection (1 Cor 11:26), but it also makes salvation so present that we can smell, touch, and taste it. The lightning of mercy strikes us. The waves of grace wash over us. We are swallowed up in the light of love.

We know that in the early centuries of the church the baptized were welcome to commune. That is true today. But the seemingly odd twist that our ancestors in the faith put on the eucharist was that no one but the baptized could be present; others could not so much as observe from the back of the room. After the sermon, the non-members, the people who had not become part of the Body of Christ via baptism, were escorted out and the doors closed behind them.

I am pretty sure I do not agree with this practice, but I do believe it points to something of extraordinary importance. Today we are so eager to be welcoming and hospitable that we tend to suggest that the communion at the Lord's table represents just another part of the "stuff" we do on Sunday mornings. We drain the mystery right out of it. There is no urgency about the fact that nothing less than salvation is both declared and made available there.

I believe those early Christians had been caught up in the mystery. They knew that in the eucharist something so deep, so real, so "now" was happening that something of the mystery needed to be preserved. When God encountered Moses in the burning bush, God instructed Moses to come no closer and to remove his sandals because he was now standing on holy ground. Something of the same was going on with those early Christians. They lived in a world where little good news, little in the way of blessings, little hope was available, but in Jesus Christ they knew they lived now in a new reality, and in that reality their Risen and Glorious Lord was present in the meal he had instituted.

What might happen to us if we were captured by that sense of mystery, by the holy things that happen in the eucharist? What if we admitted that we do not fully understand the workings of our Lord in his holy meal, but that something miraculous happens there? I wonder sometimes if we forget what happens between Jesus and us when we eat and drink in his presence. We have become so casual, so intent on being user-friendly, so cautious about offending that we have pulled the plug on what should be the high power moment of the week.

The Secret Revealed

I have a bishop acquaintance who has had a long-standing practice of removing his shoes when he is celebrating the eucharist. A bit eccentric? Perhaps, but it stands as a powerful witness to what takes place in the chancels of our churches.

One of the greatest of all eucharistic hymns states both the mystery of the holy meal and our proper response quite well.

> Let all mortal flesh keep silence, and with fear and trembling stand;
> Ponder nothing earthly minded, for with blessing in his hand
> Christ our God to earth descendeth, our full homage to demand.
> King of kings, yet born of Mary, as of old on earth he stood,
> Lord of lords in human vesture, in the Body and the Blood
> He will give to all the faithful his own self for heavenly food.
> (*The Hymnal 1982*, number 324)

Summary: The eucharist both reveals the mystery of salvation and makes it available to us.

Discussion question: In what ways are you a mystery to yourself? Is it possible for Jesus to love the parts of you that you yourself do not know?

Action item: Read 1 Cor 2. It works almost as a jazz riff on mystery. How many mysteries do you discover in that chapter?

18

Sacrifice

THE WORD "SACRIFICE" CARRIES with it a heavy load of negative connotations. In the way we ordinarily use it that word suggests giving up something we would rather keep. For instance, who has not heard a dieter complain about sacrificing chips, chocolate, or ice cream. I once heard a famous singer in a TV interview say that her favorite food was an ice cream sundae, but she also said she had not had one for fifteen years. That, indeed, was a sacrifice for the sake of her appearance.

In the history of religion sacrifice carries a more nefarious meaning. It often meant immolation for the people in the Ancient Near East. I visited the ruins of Megiddo in Israel many years ago. As we stood at the remains of the city gate our guide informed us that excavations had found the skeletal remains of several children under the structure. Part of the duty of the ancient ruler who build the gate was to offer his children as a sacrifice to win the favor of the local divinity for the city. It sent a chill through me. Later in Jerusalem we looked down into the Valley of Hinnom, where ancient inhabitants sacrificed their children by fire to appease the gods. Immolations and sacrifice functioned as the offering to divinities of what one valued most in order the gain their favor.

Sacrifice is serious business. It means giving away something of value for a higher cause.

SACRIFICE

In church history the eucharist came to be regarded as a sacrifice. This stood as one of the major points of contention between Roman Catholics and Protestants during the sixteenth century. The Protestants claimed that Roman Catholic belief stated that each mass was an act of re-sacrificing Christ. That is, each eucharist was another Calvary where Jesus was offered to God as the payment for the sins of the world. I need to add that a good deal of animus and misunderstanding was active on both sides of this argument, and that the Protestants may well have misconstrued the nuances of the Roman position. Nevertheless, the misunderstanding continues even till today, and that distorts a proper and healthy view of sacrifice.

In the best sense anything we offer to God is a sacrifice. Psalm 116 praises God for delivering the psalmist from death. The response states, "I will offer to you a thanksgiving sacrifice and call on the name of the Lord" (vs.17). Psalm 51 confesses sin and begs God for forgiveness. The psalmist notes that sorrow for sin is part of the process of reconciliation with God. "The sacrifice acceptable to God is a broken spirit, a broken and contrite heart, O God, you will not despise." Other biblical examples abound.

In the eucharist we commonly say that we offer a sacrifice of praise and thanksgiving. This takes the form of prayer, hymns, offerings of money, kneeling in the presence of God, and even the act of taking time to go to church. These are sacrifices. And we should acknowledge that none of these are as simple or as easily accomplished as they seem. To offer praise and thanksgiving to anyone, not to mention God, means that we have to step out of the center of our lives, notice what good the other has done, and find a way both to state and to act out praise.

It is easier not to notice, to continue to occupy center stage of our lives, and to keep any word of honor to ourselves; it simply costs us so much less.

The eucharist asks us to straighten out this distorted view of things. We are asked to remember the mighty and merciful things God has done for us, and then to take that fact into our self-understanding. From the center of our lives we respond by saying in effect, "You are God, and I am not." And from there we are asked to generate something that does not come easily to most people, namely, gratitude. You can sense that thanking and praising God demands that we make a spiritual journey that helps us sense where we properly stand before God. The old-fashioned language puts it quite well: "It is very meet, right, and our bounden duty, that we should at all times, and in all places, give thanks unto thee, O Lord, holy Father, almighty, everlasting God" (Book of Common Prayer, p. 333).So, then, understanding the eucharist as a sacrifice of praise and thanksgiving can become a major source of spiritual maturity and health. We need, however, to say more.

Is the eucharist in some sense a sacrifice of Christ offered to God? Are we in a way recreating the events of Calvary over and over again? This is a place where we need clarity by making some distinctions. Let me make several points.

- First, the sacrifice of Christ on the cross stands as a once-and-for-all affair. Nothing about it needs repetition or addition. The book of Hebrews says, "But as it is, [Jesus] has appeared once for all at the end of the age to remove sin by the sacrifice of himself." (9:26).

- This is one of those places where making a distinction is important. Jesus' sacrifice should not be understood as his becoming God's divine whipping boy. Rather, it is essential that we understand that God was acting in Jesus. God in Christ was offering God's self as compelling proof that God stands utterly committed to humanity. The sacrifice of the cross shows that nothing can stand in the way of God reaching out to humanity in a cosmic act of reconciliation. In a sense God in Christ is offering self to humanity in a sacrifice of love. To pursue this further, see my books *Journey with Jesus: Encountering Christ in his Birth, Baptism, Death, and Resurrection* and also *The Language of Love: A Basic Christian Vocabulary*.

- In the eucharist we stand on this side of the resurrection even as we remember the cross. Furthermore, we have been joined to the Risen Lord by our baptism into his death and resurrection. Given this we can stand before God and re-present the cross to God, in effect, saying, remember what you have done for us. Remember that you, God, have committed yourself in life and death to us. We lift up Christ and offer what he has done for us. One of the eucharistic prayers in the Book of Common Prayer states it this way: "Unite us to your Son in his sacrifice, that we may be acceptable through him" (p.369). We take what God has given us, divine forgiveness and blessing through Christ, and offer it back to God, asking that we be acceptable in and through Christ. It is not so different from the simple act of a table grace. We bless God for the food provided for us, asking that God will bless it so that we serve and bless God. There is a wonderful circularity of grace in this.

- Moreover, in the eucharist we are immersing ourselves in the death and resurrection of our Lord and Savior, offering ourselves as a sacrifice in and through Christ.

What might change for us if we were to incorporate the idea of sacrifice into our eucharistic piety? First, it would center us firmly in Jesus. One of the odd dynamics of life for me is how easily I forget him. I find that I can slip comfortably into the role of the lord of my own life and have confidence in the idea that I possess what I need to save myself. My better self knows that to be untrue, but it happens on a daily basis. The eucharist as sacrifice pulls me back to my proper center. God has offered, indeed, sacrificed, self in Christ for the sake of the world, and I take that central act of history and offer it back to God as my sacrifice.

The eucharist reminds us that we are asked to offer ourselves to God. It is easy and comfortable for us to enjoy the graciousness of God, but to make a response calls for more from us. The eucharist pulls us into this sacrificial mode of being in powerful ways. Again, consider the old-fashioned language used in a eucharistic prayer: "Here we offer and present unto thee, O Lord, our selves, our souls and bodies, to be a reasonable, holy, and living sacrifice unto thee" (*Book of Common Prayer*, p. 336). That represents a proper response to Christ's sacrifice.

The eucharist sets us up for a life of service and sacrifice. It shapes and molds us into people who are eager to offer ourselves to others in the name of Christ. And this is the lifestyle Jesus desires for us. "Whoever wishes to be great among you must be your servant, and whoever wishes to be first among you must be your slave" (Matt 20:26–27). There are many ways I can remember my parents. But for me recalling them as people of sacrifice has been important. They offered me time, worry, care, advice, discipline, and affection.

All of that required sacrifice of all they were and all they had. And I have tried to do the same for my daughters. I have offered to my parents my thanksgiving for their service by my own sacrifice to my family. It's the circle of grace. It is sacrifice, and it is God's way.

Summary: In the eucharist we offer ourselves united with Christ as a sacrifice of praise, thanksgiving, worship, and service.

Discussion question: We always need to return to Jesus. In what ways does the eucharist help you do that?

Action item: Philippians 2:6–11 represents an early Christian hymn the lifts up Jesus' sacrifice. Read it slowly. What are the elements of sacrifice noted there?

19

What Is at the End of the Road?

I LIVE IN Los Angeles, a great and sprawling city famous for its many highways and streets. Cars seems to be a necessity of life here. I was recently driving on a wide and tree-lined boulevard, and the car ahead of me began to drift in and out of my lane. I decided that safety demanded that I pass this vehicle. As I did so, I looked at the driver, and saw that he was texting, using his steering wheel to hold his phone. It shook me up a bit. By not looking ahead he could have ended both his life and mine.

It pays to keep our eyes on the road, to be aware of the future that lies before us. One of the vitally important roles of the eucharist lies in its call to keep an eye on God's future, on what lies at the end of our road.

Perhaps the most obvious way it does this comes with the Memorial Acclamation in the liturgy. This is part of many eucharistic prayers and serves as a quick summary of the good news. One common form is this: Christ has died, Christ is risen, Christ will come again. That last phrase, of course, immediately asks us to look into the future toward the end of the age and the return of Christ.

Paul affirms this in his first letter to the Corinthians. He has heard reports of various abuses of the Lord's Supper taking place in the Corinthian congregation. To address the issues he solemnly repeats the Words of Institution, the statements made by Jesus himself at the Last Supper. Then as a punch line he adds, "For as often as you eat this bread and drink this cup, you proclaim the Lord's death until he comes" (11:26). Clearly he understands the holy meal as an act that should continue until the end of the age, and he also sees that the meal thereby draws our attention to the end. The eucharist, then, asks us to remember the past as epitomized in Jesus, to receive the Risen Christ in the present, and to keep a focus on his return at the end of time.

This sense of the eucharist as a meal of the future becomes richer when we recall that in the scripture a banquet often functions as a symbol for the climax, the completion, of God's plan of salvation for the world. For instance, Luke's gospel is a gold mine of Jesus' parables, one of which concerns a great banquet (Luke 14:15–24). A man has laid out a lavish meal, but the invited guests all make bogus excuses for not attending. The man says to his servants, "Well, in that case, go out into the streets and invite the poor and infirm." The servants do so, but they also tell the man that there remain still more seats at the banquet. The master directs the servants, telling them, "Go out into the streets and twist arms and compel people to come." This parable stands as a response to a comment from a guest at a dinner party at which Jesus was a guest. The guest had said, "Blessed is anyone who will eat bread in the kingdom of God" (vs. 15). The parable suggests that the end of the age will be like a sumptuous banquet populated by a surprising group of guests.

We cannot overlook the place of a banquet in the parable of the Prodigal Son (Luke 15:11–32). When the prodigal returns to the father, reestablishing the broken ties of family, the father calls for an extravagant feast of celebration. We can read this part of the parable to suggest that it portrays the heavenly banquet in the new age when God has reconciled all things to God's self.

At this point allow me a side-step. I have spoken of the end of the age, the return of Christ, the reconciled creation, and heaven. As I read the New Testament I find little in the way of concrete detail. Even in Revelation the descriptions are highly symbolic and suggestive but hardly detailed and concrete. What comes across is not so much what heaven looks life and how it is furnished as much as a quality of life, a way of being. Indeed, in the gospel of

What Is at the End of the Road?

John heaven begins now and continues in the next age. Consider this instance: "Very truly I tell you, anyone who hears my word and believes him sent me has eternal life, and does not come under judgment, but has passed from death to life" (John 5:24). This new quality of life eternal consists of closeness to God, praising God, being transformed into the image of Christ, and joy in the loving presence of God. Moreover, death and pain have been conquered and have no power over the redeemed. I think 1 John says it remarkably well: "Beloved, we are God's children now; what we will be has not yet been revealed. What we do know is this: when he is revealed, we will be like him, for we will see him as he is" (5:3).

The eucharist works as mighty signal to keep our end in sight. We know that death does not have the last word of life, thanks to the resurrection of Jesus. In a sense, we know the end of the story. We will be gathered together around God's great banquet table, feasting on God's presence and mercy, living beyond the dominion of death and tragedy, and rejoicing that we are the people who have conquered because Christ has conquered. Is that not something to which we can look forward? Can we not face all of life with a resurrectional hope of eternal life? Don't we eagerly anticipate that when we feast at the table of the Lord here and now?

John Wesley used a wonderful image. He said that the eucharist is the antipasto course of heaven. I agree!

Summary: The eucharist provides a foretaste of the heavenly banquet in the next age.

Discussion question: What elements of the heavenly banquet are suggested by the eucharist?

Action item: The eucharist assures us that the future lies in God's hands. Make a list of the "baggage" you need to leave behind as you walk into your future with Christ.

20

The Family Meal

When our daughters were growing up my wife and I worked hard at having dinner together every night. As they became teenagers this became more difficult. Differences in schedule and tastes in food became sources of contention, and we were told that no other families had meals together. Nevertheless, we persisted. It was during the evening meal we found out what each of us had done that day, what had gone wrong, what we wanted to accomplish, and what we valued. This became a time to laugh, argue, teach, and complement. It became a place to practice putting up with each other. In a serious way we were never more a family than at the dinner table.

Holy communion serves as a common title for the eucharist. It suggests being together is a significant way. The Latin root for "communion" carries the ideas of sharing, imparting, and making something in common. If we were to commune with a friend, that does not mean idle chit-chat on the front porch, but rather a sharing so deep that an important bond is forged. This is something of what I was suggesting in the above paragraph with the image of the family meal.

It should not surprise us that the eucharist has taken the title "holy communion" to itself. In that holy meal we commune with the Risen Lord as he graces us with this presence, his body and blood, in the consecrated bread and cup. We have been born into

Christ's family in baptism, and the eucharist serves as that important, life-altering meal that we share with Jesus himself.

But it does not function only as a communion with Christ, but also as a communion with all who share in the meal. Again, in baptism we Christians have been made brothers and sisters in Christ and in the eucharist we live into that fact and we demonstrate it. The church that my wife and I attend consists of a very diverse group of people, of many races, ages, educational levels, unhoused and housed, straight and gay, rich and poor. And as we walk to the altar rail it would be hard to miss that diversity but also the fact that we are all aiming to receive our Lord together. In this way it becomes the family meal in the most significant sense.

The eucharist represents not only a communion, a making common, the various kinds of baptized persons who gather at a local church, but also people around the world, in all the time zones, who share in eucharist with us. And not just the people of the present, but also those who communed in the pasts but now need no sacrament because they dwell in the nearer presence of Christ. And we commune with all those in the future who will share with us in baptism and the sacred meal until the end of time. Moreover, it joins heaven and earth, so that we share in common with the angels, archangels, and all the host of heaven. Eucharist makes us all a gigantic family who share in the precious presence of Jesus Christ himself.

You may by now sense a problem. Does this communion include the people we have good reason to dislike? Does it include people we know to have sinned? Of course it does. We have said and done things that have rightly earned the dislike of others, and none of us can claim never to have sinned against God. We have not loved God with our whole being and as our highest priority and we have not loved neighbor as self. This is a true fact for all who commune, have communed, and ever will commune. Being a part of the Body of Christ, the church, means that we are always learning to put up with each other. But despite all that we in Christ have a bond deeper than blood, a bond that transcends all our usual distinctions. "There is no longer Jew or Greek, there is no longer slave or free, there is no longer male of female; for all of you are one in Christ Jesus" (Gal 3:28).

Years ago a group of us went to the eucharist at the Melkite Rite cathedral in Jerusalem. At that point I had heard the term "Melkite" but I did not know what it meant. Furthermore, I did not know the liturgy, the language used, the music, or any of the congregants. Over the altar a stunning fresco portrayed the Risen Christ seated in glory with his right hand raised in blessing. That I did know. And that was enough. While there was much that was unfamiliar I felt deeply connected with it all because it was focused on Christ, whose body and blood we would all receive. It was communion in every sense.

So, the eucharist demonstrates that we are a family and it actualizes that fact. If that is true, then it implies that we need to live it out in a commitment to each other. We need to act like we are united in the deepest possible sense. Jesus had something to say about this. During his last meal with his disciples Jesus said, "I give you a new commandment, that you love one another. Just as I have love you, you also should love one another. By this everyone will know that you are my disciples, if you have love for one another" (John 13:24–25). In this consists the prime directive for all the baptized.

There is more. When Jesus provides us with the bread of life and cup of salvation during the eucharist, we should sense that we have a responsibility to provide daily bread for those who have none. It would stand as a testimony against us if we did not understand the link between communion and providing for the hungry of the world. I live in Los Angeles, one of the most glamorous and wealthy cities in the world. Yet I see many hungry and homeless people on my way to church each week. I am grateful that my church has an extensive feeding program; we are a eucharistic congregation living out the implications of that. We can do no less.

One of the joys of being a priest consists of being able to administer the sacrament. I find great comfort in that and see it as a high point of my ministry. At the altar rail I can give people Jesus, even if my sermon has flopped and my pastoral work has missed the point. And it is also a place where you see people in all their diversity and need. All are unique individuals as they come forward with their needs and joys. This woman has cancer. This kid is lost and lonely. This couples live in a bad marriage. This man has just had a promotion. It is all there, laid out for Jesus to see. And he gives us his presence. And we are made one for the sake of God's mission in the world. We are family.

Summary: In the eucharist we participate in a family meal in which we are one with Christ and with each other.

Discussion question: Jesus does not erect barriers between people. How does the eucharist help us do the same?

Action item: Sketch out your plan for the altar area that of a church emphasizes the idea of family meal and communion.

21

Food for the Journey

WHEN I WAS SERVING as bishop diocesan in Montana my schedule called for me to be on the road in that vast state nearly every weekend. The purpose of these trips was to visit congregations, celebrate eucharist, preach, baptize, confirm, and meet with the priest, the parish vestry, and as many others as possible. For this introvert that required enormous reserves of energy. Sunday afternoon involved the trip back home to Helena. Almost always I had to pull over to the side of the road and take a short nap, and even then I was exhausted by the time I arrived home. And what I wanted to do was eat. I was careful to consume lots of protein for Sunday lunch and at the evening meal. Both were food for the journey, and both were essential.

At baptism we confess Jesus Christ as Lord and Savior and then we proceed to follow him in the way of love. One popular and sound image for baptismal and eucharistic living is the idea of pilgrimage. We can rightly say that we are on a journey with and toward Jesus. This is hardly a new idea. In the seventeenth century John Bunyan wrote *Pilgrim's Progress*, a sublime allegory about a man named Christian on a journey to the Heavenly City.

We, then, are making a pilgrimage, a journey, an odyssey through life with Jesus the Risen One traveling with us, guiding us, and serving as our model and our goal. And the journey can be exhausting. The writer of Hebrews knew about this. "Lift up your drooping hands and strengthen your weak knees, and make straight paths for your feet" (12:12–13). But what weakens us and tires us? The simple answer lies in the fact that we are surrounded by forces that work against us, that push us off the path, that wear us down. And they drain the energy for life from us. Finding it hard to pray can be a symptom. Not being able to care about others or finding that you do not desire God also serve as signs that we are tiring. We simply want to sit and not worry about our growth in Christ, our journey in prayer and service, or our desire to be with Jesus.

These are signs that we need to stop and eat. The eucharist provides the food we need, the food for the journey. We need to find our place at the altar and feed on the Bread of Life.

I think the energy-restoring power of the eucharist lies in these factors. First, in the holy meal we know we are drawing near to Christ and, more importantly, he is drawing near to us. We realize the power of this from human relationships. If I feel as if I am drifting away from my wife, that sends a certain message that I need to be with her. The eucharist functions in a similar way.

Moreover, the eucharist functions as an experience of the resurrection. What effect does it have on you to spend time with an energetic, charismatic, joyful person? Do you not find yourself taking on those same qualities? The Risen Christ present and available in the eucharist always shares the power of his life and love with us when we dine at his table. We can say to ourselves, "The power that conquered death is being given to me here and now in the eucharist. Jesus wants to bless me with his deathless love and life. He gives me now what I cannot find within myself." This sacred event pulls us back into the Easter reality and powers us for our journey.

Furthermore, communion functions as an act of care and support from our Lord. Imagine that you are worn down by a day of work and on an impulse you stop at the house of a friend on your way home. Your friend can read the weariness in your fact. And she responds," Sit down and let me get you a snack and something to drink." Soon tea and cookies appear, and after a bit of both you can feel life returning. Was it the food or was it the concern of your friend that served as the source of energy? The eucharist works that way, too. The Risen One gives us his own self to energize our odyssey.

Finally, the eucharist enables us to recapture the vision of life as a journey with Jesus. This holy meal draws us back to the basics of who we are and what we are called to do. For me to be a Christian person means to love Jesus, to rejoice in the Paschal mystery, to walk with him. That represents the reason I am eager to commune. It helps me re-set the program and to get rid of the clutter in my life. It is a matter of back to basics, back to Jesus.

When a person approaches the time of death they may ask to commune one last time. This is called *viaticum*, bread for the journey from this life to the next. Not just at death but along the journey, the eucharist is our bread.

"O taste and see that the LORD is good" (Ps 34:8).

Summary: The eucharist serves as the bread of life sustaining us on our journey through life.

Discussion question: How does the eucharist help empower your life?

Action item: Read Bunyan's *Pilgrim's Progress*.

22

Thank God!

THE EUCHARISTIC PRAYER FUNCTIONS as a key component of the eucharist itself in many churches. It serves as a prayer of consecration over the bread and wine. And most begin with a dialogue of ancient origin. It is called the Sursum Corda.

> Celebrant: The Lord be with you.
> People: And also with you.
> Celebrant: Lift up your hearts.
> People: We lift them to the Lord.
> Celebrant: Let us give thanks to the Lord our God.
> People: It is right to give him thanks and praise.

What follows is named the Proper Preface, and it briefly gives reasons to thank and praise God.

It begins:

> Celebrant: It is right, and a good and joyful thing, always and everywhere to give thanks to you, Father Almighty, Creator of heaven and earth.

Then comes material appropriate for the season of the liturgical year. At Christmas the incarnation of Jesus from the Virgin Mary is noted, and at Easter the glorious resurrection of the Paschal Lamb is called to mind. I have quoted material from the Book of Common Prayer, but many denominations have this or similar material.

It would be difficult to miss the point that the eucharist is about thanksgiving and gratitude for God's activity of blessing. What follows in the main body of a eucharistic prayer often lifts up God's act of creation, God's acts in Israel, and especially God's acts in Jesus' incarnation, death, and resurrection. The prayer often continues with a recitation of Jesus' words over the bread and cup at the Last Supper, followed by invocations of the Holy Spirit on the bread and wine and on those who will commune, and then it ends, as you might surmise, with a grand doxology to God.

That brings us to the origin of the word "eucharist." Its root is the Greek of the early church. The "eu" at the beginning of the word serves as a prefix that connotes something good, favorable, even cheerful. The "charis" part of the term is related to the word for grace, favor, goodwill, and joy. Putting that together we have our word "eucharist" and it carries the idea of thanksgiving for God's goodwill and favor. As you can see, it is a very positive term that implies our response to divine grace.

The whole action of God in the eucharist consists of blessing us, forgiving us, accepting us, affirming us, empowering us by granting us the presence of the Risen Lord. The whole of salvation history comes into sharp focus in this holy meal. And it calls us to react with thanksgiving and gratitude, and even gives us the words to do so. Thanksgiving is the name of this game.

All of us, however, endure times when gratitude and thanksgiving do not come easily because of the circumstances of our life. Maybe you face a financial crunch or a child has become seriously ill. We may not feel thankful, but we can practice it anyway. In the language of a previous time the Sursum Corda reminded people that giving gratitude to God was "our bounden duty." My experience suggests that an emotional crisis is exactly the best time to make the effort of giving thanks. This marks a step toward spiritual health by focusing us on God and away from our own pain.

Crisis or not, thanksgiving and gratitude stand as virtues for the baptized people of Christ. Part of the value of having an intentional commitment to eucharistic participation lies in its ability to provoke the practice of thanksgiving and gratitude. Several factors come into play.

First, gratitude and thanksgiving place us properly in the world. These virtues are based on remembering that God is God and we are not. The essence of sin, for example, consists of the basic assumption that we are the center of our world. It is a problem for every person, past, present, and future. Thanksgiving corrects that assumption by calling to mind that much of our lives consist of gifts and blessings freely given from God's hand.

Second, thanksgiving and gratitude waken the eyes of our hearts and minds. They ask us to be aware of the shape of our lives, to look beyond our own immediate thought or emotion, and to step back and observe. When we are able to do that, we may well sense that grace and blessing are key factors in our lives. We might become aware that life consists more in what we are given than in what we earn or produce. And the next small step of awareness happens when we acknowledge that the graces result from the action of God in our lives.

Third, gratitude and thanksgiving, especially of the eucharistic variety, find their roots in Israel's history, in Jesus Christ, and in the story of the church, the Body of Christ. These, then, become paradigmatic of God's actions. The scriptural story and the life of the church show us the pattern of God's acts. For example, we have spoken about the paschal mystery, the dying and rising of Christ, as one of the keys to understanding how we face the future. Gratitude happens when we learn that God acts in the lives of people in the context of time and space in order to reconcile all of the world to God's self, and that, in turn, is rooted in God choosing to be gracious to us. From death Christ manufactures life.

I believe that our journey with Christ begins with thanksgiving and gratitude. But it also comes to its climax in eucharistic thanksgiving when we lift our hearts to God and when God touches us with the presence of the Son.

Lift up your hearts!

Summary: The eucharist is both an act of thanksgiving to God and a means of sparking thanksgiving.

Discussion question: Jesus demonstrates the way God acts. How has God blessed you so that you are thankful? How could you carry that with you to the eucharist?

Action item: Do and say something in the name of Christ that will spark gratitude.

23

Revealed in the Breaking of the Bread

THE NEW TESTAMENT CONTAINS a story that will help us summarize many of the major sacramental themes we have been considering. It comes from the pen of the Bible's matchless storyteller, Luke. Let's look again in detail at the narrative about the road to Emmaus (Luke 24:13–35).

The events of the story take place on the evening of the first Easter, and we find two disciples walking from Jerusalem, the site of the resurrection, to the village of Emmaus, about seven miles from Jerusalem. This gives them two roughly two hours to chat. As they walk the Risen Lord Jesus approaches and travels with them. Luke makes an intriguing comment, that the two were kept from recognizing Jesus. Apparently they are engaged in a lively conversation and Jesus asks what they are discussing. One of the walkers named Cleopas answers the question with what has always seemed to me to be a sarcastic tone. He says, "You must be so out of it that you are the only person who has not heard about the reports regarding Jesus." Then Jesus feigns ignorance, asking "What things?" Cleopas replies that Jesus was a great prophet who had been crucified, that they had hoped he would be the longed-for leader who would redeem Israel, and that now some of his disciples were saying that they had had a vision of angels telling them that Jesus was alive and that, in fact, they had found his tomb empty.

Here the tone of the narrative changes. Jesus chides them for being so slow believe and for not understanding what the Hebrew scriptures say about him. Then Jesus interprets those scriptures in terms of his own life, death, and resurrection. I can guess that most of the two-plus hours of walking must have been spent on this exercise. And I am also be jealous of them having a Bible study led by Jesus himself!

They approach Emmaus and the two invite Jesus to supper because evening was approaching. The story then jumps to the climax as we find Jesus and the two at the table. Certain details are carefully stated. Jesus took bread, blessed it, broke it, and gave it to them. And at that moment they recognized him. And suddenly he is no longer there.

Despite the approaching darkness the two disciples hurry back to Jerusalem and report to the eleven apostles and the others. "Yes," the apostles reply. "The Lord is risen and he has appeared to Simon Peter." Then the two make their report. Note carefully the two factors in their witness: that their hearts burned within them as Jesus opened the scriptures to them, and that they had recognized him in the breaking of the bread. The story per se ends there, but Luke's narrative continues by telling us that as the group were discussing this among themselves, the Risen Jesus appears among them. Can you imagine the awe, questioning, fear, faith, and praise that appearance must have evoked?

This story clearly reflects the worship of the early church. Jesus speaks in and through the scriptures, and he reveals his presence during the holy meal. For the past two millenia this has remained the pattern of Sunday worship: word and sacrament. The early Christians adapted the synagogue service of the reading of scripture, sermon, and prayers to their own setting, and the events of the Last Supper shaped their celebrations of the holy meal.

Allow me to make a few comments based on this beautiful story. Regarding the word of scripture, remember that Jesus himself functions as the interpreter. In the story he seems a bit irritated that the disciples, good Jewish people who knew their Bible, had failed to understand its proper meaning. Jesus here establishes for us the interpretive principle that we should use in reading the Bible:

read it through Jesus. His life, death, resurrection, ascension, and promise of coming again function as the reading glasses we need to understand properly the Bible. The biblical message points to Jesus, explains Jesus, calls us to faithful obedience to Jesus, and secures our future in Jesus.

This, then, calls us to the spiritual discipline of Bible study and prayer. I am not certain how we can maintain a healthy and maturing relationship with our Savior unless we read the Bible, study it, and pray over it. I certainly understand that the Bible is not easy reading, and that is why it is best done in a group with the help of aids such as good study Bibles. I would add that most of the important things in life are not easy and require effort and discipline. One of my favorite Old Testament episodes regards Jacob's wrestling match with a mysterious night-time being, likely an angel, at the brook Jabbok (Gen 32:22–32). They wrestled through the night, and as dawn was approaching, Jacob held down the angel, demanding a blessing. Working with the Bible can feel like a wrestling match, but if we hold on we will be given a blessing.

Regarding the holy meal in the Emmaus story remember the detail of Jesus taking, blessing, breaking, and giving the bread. These constitute the four-fold action of the eucharist. Bread and wine are offered, they are blessed, the bread is broken and wine poured, and then they are distributed. Some say we should regard these as the four acts that constitute the sacrament of the altar. In a more practical sense, I am inspired by our repeating of actions that go back to Jesus himself. This helps me feel connected both with Jesus and with our ancestors in the faith.

In my own church the breaking of the bread, called the Fraction, comes as an especially solemn moment, The eucharist prayer and the Lord's Prayer have both been recited, and now the bread, often lifted up, is broken. A moment of silence follows, and then a portion of scripture is either read or sung. It recalls, of course, the breaking of Christ's body on the cross and the way in which we participate in that when we consume a portion of the broken bread. The spiritual asks "Were you there when they crucified my Lord?" And at this moment we can reply, "We were. And we are."

The bread is broken so that it can be shared. But the sharing does not end with the dismissal at the end of the liturgy. We share the bread of life when we witness to the love of God in Christ to the world. This is the work of evangelism and stands as a basic element of our faith. Christianity is by nature a missionary religion; we share the bread with the world in this way. I think we should regard it as a privilege and honor to do so.

We also share the bread of life when we feed the hungry. It would demonstrate a profound lack of integrity if we were to share the bread in the eucharist but failed to share our daily bread with the multitudes who need food and so much else. Christianity is by nature an incarnational religion; we have the privilege and honor of making real the love of Christ for the world.

Finally, let me make a comment about Cleopas and his companion. We do not know who that second disciple was but given that no name is used we might well assume that the other person was a woman. They were both from Jerusalem and disciples of Jesus. That certainly suggests that they were people of the covenant, Jewish people. It reminds us that Jesus was Jewish and that our faith is deeply rooted in that religion. To be a baptized believer and to be anti-sematic is impossible.It also reminds us that baptism constitutes us as people of the covenant. When we hear the story of Cleopas and his companion we join them in their journey. The scriptures of the covenant are interpreted and we recognize Jesus' presence in the breaking of the bread. Emmaus is our story, too.

The actual site of Emmaus remains uncertain. Four possible locations have been suggested. One of those is the town of Abu Ghosh. Benedictine monks have a monastery there and it includes a stunning twelfth century church built by the crusaders. Composed of white stone, its interior walls still contain crusader frescoes decorating the gothic arches. The monks use it to this day for their daily round of worship. One of the great honors of my life came as an invitation to celebrate the eucharist there. I vividly remember walking into that holy space on my way to the altar. I began, "Blessed be God, Father, Son, and Holy Spirt," and time collapsed. Cleopas and his friend were there. And so was Jesus. It changed everything. It still does.s

Revealed in the Breaking of the Bread

Summary: The Risen Christ reveals himself in the breaking of the bread.

Discussion question: Imagine Jesus as your Bible teacher. What would you most need to hear from him?

Action item: Take a walk with a friend. Imagine Jesus with you. What feelings occur? What thoughts do you carry away from the event?

www.ingramcontent.com/pod-product-compliance
Lightning Source LLC
Chambersburg PA
CBHW070312100426
42743CB00011B/2440